SIR WILLIA
NORTHE..N TOUR
1758

Edited and introduced by
John G. Dunbar

TUCKWELL PRESS

in association with
The European Ethnological Research Centre
and the National Museums of Scotland

Sources in Local History No. 6

First published in 1997 in Great Britain by
Tuckwell Press Ltd
The Mill House
Phantassie
East Linton East Lothian EH40 3DG

ISBN 1 898410 98 4

British Library Cataloguing-in-Publication Data
A catalogue record for this book is available
on request from the British Library

Typeset by Carnegie Publishing
Printed and bound by
Cromwell Press, Broughton Gifford, Melksham, Wiltshire

CONTENTS

Illustrations	vi
Preface	vii
Introduction	1
The Journal	23
Notes	132
Index	137

v

ILLUSTRATIONS

Maps   2, 3

Sir William Burrell   4

Drumlanrig Castle   47

Inveraray Castle   81

Dunstaffnage Castle   87

Elgin Cathedral   103

Glamis Castle   110

Tynemouth Monastery   125

Preface

With this publication of William Burrell's Tour of 1758, the European Ethnological Research Centre (EERC) broadens the scope covered by its Sources in Local History series. So far it has concentrated on the publication of the texts of diaries and account books, since these have been relatively little explored by researchers, and since there is an international movement to study them. Publications so far have been of documents of a highly personal nature, which had more to do with their own localities than with overviews of wider regions. The EERC will continue to publish such sources, to provide material for future research work by scholars of various kinds, but it will also take on board sources like the present one.

This, an early and detailed account of journeying on horseback in Scotland before the concept of tourism was known, throws a great deal of light on the various localities that William Burrell visited. In some ways it is a positive virtue that he was an Englishman, since he was able to set his English background off against what he saw in Scotland, and this makes comparison possible. Even at the simple level of wallpaper being used in Kelso houses, as in England, but not elsewhere (to his knowledge) in Scotland, we learn something of the impact of the Border situation. In a similar way, at a later date in the eighteenth century, Johnson and Boswell commented from time to time on comparisons between the food of the Scots and the food of the English. It is in this kind of way, cumulatively, that indicators of national identity or characteristics can come to the fore.

Burrell was an acute observer, with an eye to the economics of farming and food-prices, and we learn a great deal about such matters. Turnips, for example, were already being grown in rows in the neighbourhood of Glasgow, and the potato business was flourishing in the neighbourhood of Edinburgh.

Like most other travellers, he commented fairly regularly on the nature of his accommodation, mostly at inns, and a good picture of the facilities for travellers can be got. Equally, there are interesting details about the food available. For example, in south-west Scotland they had boiled eggs and Cheshire cheese, with tea, for breakfast and the eggs at least are in line with the comments of many other travellers, some of whom despaired about the quality of Scottish cooking, and depended very largely on boiled eggs, not so much for breakfast as for other meals. Chicken broth is mentioned, and at various times there was sour milk and goats' whey and buttermilk to drink.

But Burrell was not only concerned with things of the stomach and of economics. He also commented extensively on important buildings and structures, and on life at the universities of Glasgow, Edinburgh, and St Andrews, as well as giving full accounts of paintings to be found in these seats of learning. He obviously had an eye for the aesthetic.

This is not an outstanding work of literature, but it is of great historical value, providing comments on different localities – in England and Ireland as well as in Scotland – that are not available elsewhere, and the work in general helps to fill in gaps in the record of history. John Dunbar is to be greatly congratulated on his painstaking work in transcribing the text from the manuscript in the National Library of Scotland, and on annotating the document so fully. It is a worthy addition to the Sources in Local History series, and should be the forerunner to many more.

Alexander Fenton

Introduction

Banff
Inverness
Grantown
Aberdeen
Fort William
Dalnacardoch
Dundee
Perth
St. Andrews
Stirling
Edinburgh
Glasgow
Berwick upon Tweed
Ayr
Kelso
Dumfries
Alnwick
Giants Causeway
Newcastle
Tynemouth
Antrim
Port Patrick
Carlisle
Chester le Street
Belfast
Durham
Donaghadee
Stockton
Whitby
Richmond
Helmsley
Scarborough
Boroughbridge
Malton
York
Beverley
Hull
Doncaster
Lincoln
Grantham
Huntingdon
Royston
London

$\mathcal{N}$

Map showing route travelled by William Burrell and his party between
early July and late October 1758.

Sir William Burrell's Northern Tour 1758

Map showing William Burrell's route in more detail.

Sir William Burrell. Engraved portrait by Philip Audinet. (*Reproduced by permission of the Trustees of the National Library of Scotland*)

William Burrell was a member of a prominent landed and mercantile family settled mainly in Sussex and Kent. His father, Peter Burrell of Beckenham, Kent, was MP for Haslemere for more than thirty years and his elder brother, another Peter, was likewise an assiduous Parliamentarian.

William Burrell himself was born in 1732 and educated at Westminster School and St John's College, Cambridge. As a younger son, he had to find a profession and after qualifying LLB in 1755 he was admitted an Advocate at Doctors' Commons in 1760, in which year he also took his LLD degree. Burrell practised chiefly in the Admiralty Court, but also became Chancellor of the diocese of Worcester and subsequently of Rochester. In 1768 he entered Parliament, holding the family seat of Haslemere for six years before vacating it on acceptance of a Commissionership of the Excise. Burrell's personal appearance is known from contemporary portraits. He was described by his friend William Cole, the Cambridge antiquary, as 'an active, stirring man; a good Antiquary. He is rather low, and squints a little; but very ingenious, and scholar-like'.

The Burrells had a reputation for making fortunate marriages and William was no exception in this respect. A year after his marriage to Sophia, daughter of Charles Raymond, a banker, in 1773 his father-in-law was created a baronet with reversion of the title to William and his heirs. To the considerable wealth acquired through his marriage, therefore, Burrell in due course added a baronetcy, succeeding his father-in-law as 2nd Bt. of Valentine House, Essex, in 1789. Moreover, his wife possessed talent as well as wealth, being widely acknowledged as a gifted poetess and dramatist.

Two years before he succeeded to the baronetcy Burrell suffered a severe stroke which compelled him to withdraw from public life. He had hoped to spend his retirement completing his history of the county of Sussex, upon which he had been engaged for many years, but ill-health denied him the satisfaction of bringing the work to publication and at his death in 1796 the fruits of his labours, in the shape of fifteen volumes of manuscripts and eight large folio volumes of drawings, passed to the British Museum. Burrell died at Deepdene, Dorking, where he had spent his final years, but he was buried at West Grinstead, Sussex. There are monuments to him by Flaxman both there and at the earlier Burrell seat of Cuckfield in the same county. The family connection with Sussex continues to the present day and the baronetcy is currently held by one of Sir William's direct descendants.[1]

Burrell's researches into the history of Sussex were the culmination of a lifelong interest in historical and antiquarian studies of which the journal of his Scottish tour is the earliest known manifestation. The journal contains no direct evidence as to its date and authorship, but it offers a number of clues from which this information can be elicited. The manuscript bears the bookplate of Sir Walter Wyndham Burrell of West Grinstead (William's grandson), who died in 1886, and the preliminary leaves incorporate the initials WB and the inscription 'Given to Sophia Burrell'. Correlation of the days of the week with the days of the month, coupled with references to certain known events,[2] points to 1758 as the year of compilation, and the author's account of his reception at Inveraray, where the travellers were accorded the freedom of the burgh, can be matched to an entry in the burgh records for 2nd September of that year, which identifies the party as William Burrell Esq., John Symonds Esq., William Beal, servant, and John Swan, servant.[3]

The only time that Burrell's travelling companion, 'Mr Symonds', is mentioned by name in the journal is the occasion of their initial rendezvous at Huntingdon. No indication is given of Symonds' identity, but it is possible that he was the John Symonds, son of the Rev. John Symonds, vicar of Dullingham and Stetchworth, Cambridgeshire, who went up to St John's College, Cambridge, at the same time as Burrell. The younger Symonds was ordained in 1754 and subsequently served as curate at Stetchworth before getting a living of his own.[4] Perhaps the two young men – Burrell celebrated his twenty-sixth birthday during the tour while Symonds was a few months older – kept up a college friendship by occasionally travelling together. Certainly Huntingdon would have been the obvious place to meet on the road north had Symonds been coming from Cambridgeshire.

Another puzzle is the identity of the person referred to by Burrell when he remarks that on the first day of the tour he had no opportunity of making such observations 'as either my own genius or a desire to execute your injunctions prompted me to' (p. 25). In view of Burrell's comparative youth it might be supposed that the objectives of the tour would have been shaped by parental advice, but his father had died two years previously. More probably Burrell's mentor was drawn from his circle of professional and antiquarian associates, the most likely candidate being the well-known civil lawyer and antiquary Andrew Coltee Ducarel (1713–85).

While still an undergraduate, Burrell had been recommended to Ducarel as a promising antiquary by Dr. John Taylor, Fellow of St John's, who also helped to secure Burrell's admission as a Fellow of the Society of Antiquaries of London as early as April 1754. As well as being a prominent figure in the Society of Antiquaries, Ducarel was a senior member of Doctors' Commons and his friendship with Burrell may have deepened as the latter prepared for his own admission there.[5] Ducarel had been accustomed to spend the month of August on an antiquarian excursion through some part of England in the company of his friend Samuel Gale (1682–1754), the first Treasurer of the

Society of Antiquaries. They travelled *incognito*, accompanied by a coachman and footman, covering about fifteen miles a day and generally putting up at inns. They took with them a set of maps and a copy of Camden's *Britannia*, and each evening after dinner they wrote up their notes on the various sites visited during the course of the day.[6] Reading Burrell's journal, it is evident that his pattern of travel mirrored that of Ducarel and Gale in almost every particular – perhaps even including the choice of the *Britannia* as a *vade mecum* – and it seems more than likely that it was Ducarel whose methods of study Burrell was seeking to emulate. Another of Ducarel's correspondents who was in the habit of making summer antiquarian tours at this period was Archdeacon (later Bishop) Pococke, who had already made two short excursions into southern Scotland.[7]

Just why Burrell decided to visit Scotland is uncertain. Perhaps the novelty and challenge of such an expedition appealed to him, for Scotland had not yet become the fashionable goal of English and Continental travellers, and the Highlands, in particular, were seldom visited. Few maps or handbooks were available to the prospective visitor to that region, and the promised network of government roads was still in the making. Burrell's interests were wide-ranging and a tour of Scotland would enable him not only to explore little-known antiquities, but also to observe current developments in agriculture, industry and military engineering (where there was much activity in the aftermath of the 'Forty Five) and to visit the many new and improved seats of the nobility and gentry, some of them well stocked with paintings and other works of art. The English section of the tour may also have been devised in part to take in places associated with the Burrell family (pp. 27, 123), while in Beverley Burrell visited the (unoccupied) residence of his old schoolfellow, Sir Charles Hotham.[8] As if all this was not enough, he also decided to see a little of Ireland by interrupting the proposed coastal tour of Galloway in order to spend a few days in Down and Antrim.

Certainly Burrell's itinerary was an ambitious one. Leaving London on 8 July and joining Symonds the following evening, he travelled via Lincoln to Hull, crossing the Humber at Barton and visiting several country seats, including Burghley and Belvoir, *en route*. The party then proceeded to Beverley, York and Scarborough, making an excursion to Castle Howard on the way. From Scarborough they continued up the east coast to Stockton and Durham and thence via Lumley Castle to Chester-le-Street and on to Carlisle, making use of the new military road along the line of the Roman wall.

Entering Scotland near Annan some time during the last week of July (Burrell seldom dated his journal entries), the party proceeded via Dumfries and Newton Stewart to Portpatrick, where they took the packet boat to Donaghadee. One of the chief objects of the Irish excursion was to visit the Giant's Causeway, which made a great impression on Burrell, but they also managed to see the towns of Belfast, Antrim and Bally-money. Returning to Portpatrick by the same route, the party then skirted the Clyde coast northwards to Ayr, where Burrell came under suspicion of being a spy and was obliged to satisfy the local regimental commander as to his credentials. Once this misunderstanding had been cleared up, the travellers continued their journey via Irvine and Largs to Greenock, arriving on 10 August. Another stage brought them to Glasgow, where they seem to have spent a couple of days, showing particular interest in the cathedral and university, one of their guides apparently being the celebrated economist, Adam Smith.

From Glasgow Burrell made a short excursion to Hamilton to see the Duke of Hamilton's palace and its collections and then set out northwards to Kilsyth and Stirling. Beyond Stirling they made their first acquaintance with the Highlands, passing through Crieff and Glen Almond to visit the Earl of Bread-albane's recently enlarged house at Taymouth and then traversing 'disagreable mountainous country' to reach Blair Castle, the seat of the Duke of Atholl. From Blair the party turned southwards for Perth and Edinburgh, visiting several country houses, including Scone Palace and Hopetoun House, on their way to the capital. In Edinburgh Burrell made, or renewed, the acquaintance of several local notabilities, including the Earl of Haddington and Lord Aberdour, heir of the Earl of Morton, who invited the party to spend a couple of days at his father's nearby seat of Dalmahoy.

The party then headed for the West Highlands, repassing Glasgow and travelling north via Dumbarton and Loch Lomond to Inveraray. On the way they climbed Ben Lomond and all except Burrell, who became dizzy and had to crawl down on all fours, picnicked on the summit. It was the custom in Inveraray to confer the freedom of the burgh on distinguished visitors and, as already noted, Burrell, Symonds and their respective servants were all made freemen and burgesses. Having visited the castle, the travellers turned north again, sampling a short stretch of the new military road to Tyndrum before crossing Loch Awe and Loch Etive by ferry and making their way through Appin. From there they had planned to visit Iona, but in the event only Symonds did so, Burrell excusing himself on account of the bad weather. The journal therefore lacks any first-hand account of Iona, incorporating instead a description of the island's antiquities compiled by a local schoolmaster a few years previously (p. 90 n.10). Burrell was the earliest traveller to use this account and his version differs in some respects from those subsequently retailed by Pococke and Bishop Forbes.

Resuming their journey northwards on or about 10 September, the party travelled up the Great Glen to Inverness by way of Fort William and Fort Augustus, making good time along the military road. The travellers' interest in military affairs was further gratified by visits to the battlefield of Culloden, fought only twelve years previously, and to the new Fort George then under construction at Ardersier. After making a detour south to see Castle Grant and the timber-producing industry at Abernethy, they continued along the Moray coast via Forres and Elgin to Banff, where they visited Duff House and received the freedom of the burgh.

At this point the party turned to commence the long journey south, visiting Aberdeen and its two colleges and then travelling down the east coast via Montrose, Brechin and Forfar to Glamis. In that neighbourhood they spent the best part of a week, during which they visited Lord Strathmore's seats at Glamis and Castle Huntly, as well as the ruins of Arbroath Abbey; they also attempted to decipher the carvings on the celebrated Pictish stones at Meigle and climbed up to the prehistoric fort on Denoon Law. By now autumn was advancing, the nights were becoming frosty and the distant Grampian hills had already received their first covering of snow. On 14 October, therefore, they again turned south, now travelling more rapidly than before.

Crossing the Tay estuary at Dundee, they headed for St Andrews and then skirted the Fife coast to Kinghorn, where they embarked for Leith. After spending the night of 16 October in Edinburgh, they set out for Roslin Chapel, visiting this, as well as the neighbouring seats of Newbattle and Dalkeith, before pausing at Haddington. Much of the following day was spent making an excursion to the Bass Rock by fishing boat, after which the party rode via Soutra and Lauderdale to Melrose and Kelso. On 20 October they recrossed the Border at Coldstream and headed for Tynemouth, visiting Alnwick Castle and Seaton Delaval *en route*. Spending only an hour in Newcastle, but pausing briefly to inspect the Lumley tombs at Chester-le-Street, they continued via Bishop Auckland to Richmond and thence to Ripon, where they seem to have arrived about 24 October having visited several country seats, including Rokeby and Studley Royal on the way. Burrell says little about the final stages down the Great North Road to London, where he probably arrived just before the end of October. He does record the total distance travelled, however, namely 2535½ miles, giving a daily average (including sea crossings) of about 22 miles, which may be compared with Pococke's daily average of about 16 miles during his rather longer tour of 1760.[9]

Virtually the whole journey was made on horseback, although we hear of one occasion on which bad weather compelled Burrell and Symonds (but presumably not their servants) to take a post chaise (p. 34). No doubt the travellers took their own horses, including some spare mounts, with them, as Celia Fiennes had done half a century earlier,[10] for in the more remote parts of the country, at least, none would have been available for hire. To ascend the lower slopes of Ben Lomond, however, Burrell found it prudent to borrow a pony.

About these details of the tour Burrell has little to say, but he frequently comments on the state of the roads. The new military roads invariably win his praise, that from Newcastle to Carlisle being 'one of the finest for the length and goodness of it in England'. Indeed, his itinerary through the Highlands was evidently planned with a view of making maximum use of the military road network so far as it then existed, and he seems to have carried a copy of Andrew Rutherford's recently published roadmap with him (p. 66 n.8). Away from the military roads and turnpikes, however, the going was often difficult, whether in the English Midlands (p. 28) or the Scottish Highlands (p. 85). In some parts of the country landowners were prepared to make their own contribution to the road system and Sir Ludovic Grant is commended for building several miles of link road on Speyside, 'a work that will be highly serviceable to travellers'.

The party generally stayed at inns, those in England and northern Ireland usually attracting little comment and those in Scotland receiving rather more praise than the remarks of other travellers would lead us to expect. The New Inn at Edinburgh accommodated both men and horses 'extremely well', while the King's Arms at Dumfries was 'the best in Scotland – the accommodation good'. That at Newton Stewart, however, was dirty and flea-ridden and the landlord dishonest, a defect that he shared with his counterpart at Harlow Hill in Northumberland. In the Highlands the inns were often mere huts, offering little but whisky and oatbread (p. 95), but these deficiencies were more than remedied by the hospitality of the local gentry. Prior to their ascent of Ben Lomond the laird of Blairvockie offered the travellers sour milk and goats' whey, 'more acceptable to us than all the dainties of a palace'; he also made sure that a meal of chicken and potatoes was waiting for them on their return. At Lochnell House, in Lorn, Sir Duncan Campbell received Burrell and his companion 'with the utmost hospitality, civility and politeness', and a similar reception awaited them at Airds, where Burrell was also presented with an Irish wolfhound, a type of dog for which he had searched in vain in Ireland.

Burrell has nothing to say directly about the way in which he compiled his journal, but it seems likely that the neatly written and stylishly presented version that has come down to us represents a fair copy made from draft notes following his return. For the most part, however, the information that he gives appears to be based on his own observations and enquiries. These he evidently pursued methodically, as in his practice of collecting statistical information about local agriculture and industry and collating the results of his enquiries in a separate section at the end of the journal. Indeed, it was Burrell's anxiety to gain first-hand information that was his undoing at Ayr, where his apprehension as a spy was the direct result of the mayor (i.e. provost) 'seeing me writing in the street and making observations'. Likewise we may reasonably assume that the dimensions of antiquities that he includes are in most cases the record of his own measurements, because at Arbroath Abbey he notes that the unevenness of the ground prevented him from taking exact dimensions.

When authentic information was already available in published form, however, Burrell was not averse to making use of it, either with or without acknowledgement. One of the authorities several times referred to is Camden's *Britannia*, the edition cited apparently being that published by Gibson in 1695, and Burrell's account of his visit to Guisborough Priory suggests that he carried a copy of this work with him. Two references are made to Alexander Gordon's *Itinerarium Septentrionale* of 1726, one of them in such a way as to suggest that the volume was consulted only when Burrell was preparing the final version of his journal after his return,[11] and the same is probably true of his references to the works of Stukeley and Horsley.

It also seems likely that Burrell incorporated certain other material from Gordon, for example in his accounts of Sueno's Stone, Forres and the round tower at Brechin, without acknowledging his source. But the most noticeable instance of borrowing concerns Defoe's *Tour*, one of the few guidebooks then available to travellers. It looks very much as if Burrell carried a copy of the fourth edition of 1742 with him, occasionally using it as a source of inspiration when words or memory failed. This is particularly obvious in the description of Edinburgh and in the accounts of his visits to Drumlanrig Castle, St Andrews and the Bass Rock.

The diversity of the topics commented upon in the journal demonstrates the very wide spectrum of Burrell's interests, some of which evidently reflect his background as a member of an established landed family. His practice of systematically recording local land prices and agricultural wage rates at the principal places through which he passed (e.g. pp. 54–5, 128–9) has already been alluded to. In addition he frequently mentions the price of provisions and lists the crops, commenting an any farming practices that struck him as unusual. Between Paisley and Glasgow he saw turnips growing, 'the first we saw in Scotland', and at Boroughbridge he notes a rather laborious method of extracting rape oil. In Appin the first crop of hay was being cut in early September, while near Morpeth it was still in the field on the 22nd of that month. The growing number of enclosures on both sides of the Border frequently provoked comment and Burrell somehow managed to gain the impression that the Scots called such features 'polishes' (p. 74), a mistake perhaps caused by a highlander's pronunciation of the word 'policies'!

In his comments on planting Burrell, as we might expect, tends to be critical of the formal landscape designs of the early part of the century. The gardens at Hopetoun were 'miserably laid out, without the least taste', while Lumley was 'too much crouded with avenues which hide the prospect of a noble stream'. At Castle Stair he recognised the potentiality for creating a more natural and informal layout and his visit to Taymouth seems to have coincided with the introduction of such ideas there,[12] the great variety of trees and shrubs being planted along the winding riverside walks particularly attracting his attention.

Burrell's eye for detail is nowhere more apparent than in his observations on manufactures and commerce. In many of the towns through which he passed he describes local trades and industries at some length, sometimes, as at Greenock and Montrose, providing a good deal more information than Defoe. His account of Glasgow also contains valuable descriptions of the university and of the academy of arts recently founded by the Foulis brothers. Elsewhere he found time to record a variety of industrial processes, including the manufacture of woad at Honington, the alum works at Whitby and a combined saltpan and lime works at Belfast.

Burrell also took an interest in the state of the principal fortifications that lay along his route, displaying rather more knowledge of this subject than might be expected of a young London lawyer. At Scarborough, for example, the travellers' visit coincided with the appearance off the coast of a marauding French privateer, and Burrell describes how a signal was at once sent to all ships warning them to keep within range of the neighbouring shore battery. He was critical of the condition of the defences at Carlisle and Stirling Castle and felt that Fort Augustus, where the party was entertained by the governor, was 'rather to be considered as a neat barrack than a fortification'. The new Fort George made a much more favourable impression and Burrell's very comprehensive description benefits from the fact that the works were at that time only half finished, enabling him to examine the actual mode of construction. In particular he notes the building methods employed to make the casemates proof against mortar bombs, a process which involved the use of a special cement and alternate layers of stone, clay and earth as cladding.

Of all the topics that engaged Burrell's attention, however, those that evidently interested him most were antiquities, art and architecture, and his observations on these subjects are among the most valuable sections of the journal. He seems to have been more confident in dealing with medieval remains than with prehistoric, Roman and early historic antiquities, being more inclined in these latter fields to refer to existing authorities such as Stukeley and Gordon (pp. 25, 108). Burrell fully shared in the revived appreciation of Gothic architecture that had become fashionable during the second quarter of the eighteenth century, but unlike many of his contemporaries his approach was empirical rather than romantic. His accounts of buildings such as Arbroath and Melrose Abbeys therefore tend to be painstaking, but rather dull, blow-by-blow descriptions now important chiefly for their factual content. His stylistic preference was for mid and late Gothic of a fairly ornate character. Durham Cathedral had 'little to recommend it but its antiquity', but Beverley Minster was 'a most beautyfull Gothick building, worthy the attention of every traveller'.

Burrell was particularly interested in contemporary architecture, including interior decoration, and his accounts of country houses such as Taymouth, Blair and Scone complement those of Pococke, often adding new information. In some cases, such as Inveraray Castle, Burrell's description is the earliest that we have, while his lengthy account of Hopetoun House, compiled while the interior was still being fitted up to the designs of John and Robert Adam, is much the best to have come down to us.[13] He also had a keen eye for books and pictures. The library at Durham gets higher marks than the cathedral itself, and at Newbattle House the pictures are accorded a detailed description, while the house 'is old and not worthy notice'. Burrell's observations on paintings are clearly based on wide personal knowlege and show considerable discernment. This expertise may, in part, have been acquired through familiarity with his own family collections, for at the Bishop of Durham's palace at Bishop Auckland he recognised a picture of which the original was 'in the collection of Mr Raymond at Langley in Kent' – Burrell's own maternal uncle.

Burrell's interest in buildings was not confined to polite architecture. On several occasions he mentions the existence of mud-walled cottages, noting that many of those in the Solway area had neither chimneys nor windows. Those that did have windows had sashes (of a rather primitive kind) rather than casements, a practice which he seems to have observed elsewhere in Scotland, but not in northern Ireland or (presumably) England. At Kelso he was surprised to find that the houses had rooms lined with wallpaper, as in England. Other local customs that he comments on include washing clothes with the feet,[14] the peculiarities of highland burials and wakes, the Galloway practice of serving boiled eggs and Cheshire cheese with the breakfast tea and the curious fact that 'at Hull the women wear an odd kind of straw bonnet which makes them appear extremely frightfull'!

Tourism scarcely touched Scotland before the middle of the eighteenth century. Of the 110 or so travellers who visited the country between 1750 and 1800 and whose journals have come down to us, Burrell was one of the earliest, preceding Bishop Forbes by four years and Thomas Pennant by more than a decade.[15] He was also one of the most enterprising. Although he spent only about twelve weeks in Scotland, Burrell managed to see virtually the whole country south of the Great Glen, including parts of the Highlands to which no previous visit is recorded. His appetite for information was insatiable and the facts and figures that he so assiduously compiled furnish a unique insight into Scottish (and northern English) social and economic conditions during a period for which such data are hard to come by. In general Burrell's attitudes and opinions are those that might be expected from a serious-minded young Englishman of his class, but his observations on antiquities are unusually well informed and his comments on art and architecture reveal both taste and knowledge. Whatever the topic he is dealing with, Burrell always writes with precision, and his unaffected narrative style, occasionally enlivened by anecdote, carries the reader along without effort. If Burrell's journal is hardly substantial enough to win its author a place in the front rank of eighteenth-century travellers, it is certainly essential reading for anyone seeking to understand Scotland in the years after the 'Forty Five.

The manuscript of Burrell's journal was purchased by the National Library of Scotland in 1939 (MS 2911). It comprises a contemporary calf-bound notebook (163mm × 205mm) containing 5 preliminary leaves and 47 numbered folios followed by several blanks. The leaves containing the journal (ff. 1–41), which alone are printed here, are ruled with ink margins, the mileage figures being inserted in the left-hand margins and the running totals at the top of each leaf. Folios 42^v–44 contain a summary of economic statistics abstracted from the journal, f. 45 contains details of the inscriptions at Castle Howard and ff. 45^v and 46 contain copies of two Jacobite letters of 1746 possibly made available to Burrell by Donald Campbell of Airds; these are printed in Stewart, John H. J. and Stewart, Duncan, *The Stewarts of Appin* (1880), 173–5. Folio 46^v also contains 'a receipt to clean smutty wheat given me by Mr Tulloch of Logie'. Folio

47 contains a short glossary, together with a list of noblemen's seats in Scotland forfeited after the Jacobite rebellion, and f. 47^v contains the start of a list of Scottish trees and plants.

In preparing the manuscript for publication, the original spelling has been retained, but punctuation, capitalisation and paragraphing have been amended where necessary for purposes of clarity. In most cases abbreviations and contractions have been silently expanded when there is no doubt as to their meaning. Expansion involving some degree of conjecture is indicated by square brackets [ ]. Contractions for pounds, shillings and pence have been retained and regularised. Obvious mistakes have been silently corrected and footnotes and marginal notes have been brought into the text, except for the marginal mileage figures which are generally duplicated in the text. Material not in the manuscript, but inserted for purposes of identification is indicated by pointed brackets < >.

For their grant of permission to publish I am grateful both to the Trustees of the National Library of Scotland, as owners of the manuscript, and to Sir Raymond Burrell Bt. and C. R. Burrell Esq., as owners of copyright. Dr Iain Gordon Brown of the Department of Manuscripts of the National Library of Scotland has facilitated my research there and offered valuable advice. Professor Sandy Fenton has encouraged the idea of publication and the Hon. Simon Howard, Castle Howard; David Lockwood, Dumfries Museum; Bernard Nurse, Society of Antiquaries of London; and Professor Christopher Smout, University of St Andrews, have kindly and promptly answered specific enquiries. My greatest debt, however, is to my sister, Mary Dunbar, who not only researched the English section of the tour, but also provided much of the background information for the biographical sketch of William Burrell. The engravings in the text are reproduced by courtesy of the Royal Commission on the Ancient and Historical Monuments of Scotland. The maps were drawn by Jane Siddall.

NOTES

1. Burrell's life is outlined in the *Dictionary of National Biography* and Burke's *Peerage*. See also *Cambridge University: St John's College Admissions*, part 3, 1715–67 (1903), 129, 591–2; *The Record of Old Westminsters*, i (1928), 145; *The History of Parliament. The House of Commons 1754–1790*, ii (1964), 160–3; Cooper, Wilbraham V., *A History of the Parish of Cuckfield* (1912), 102–9; Borrowman, Robert, *Beckenham, Past and Present* (1910), *passim;* Horsfield, Thomas W., *The History, Antiquities and Topography of the County of Sussex* (1835), ii, 250 and facing plate; Williamson, George C., *Andrew and Nathaniel Plimer, Miniature Painters* (1903), 47 and plate. Cole's description of Burrell is cited by John Nichols in his *Literary Anecdotes of the Eighteenth Century*, ix (1815), 797.

2. E.g. the minority of the 2nd Earl of Massarene, the erection of an observatory at Glasgow University and the erection of the Edinburgh Royal Exchange.

3. [Beaton, Elizabeth A. and MacIntyre, Sheila W., eds.], *The Burgesses of Inveraray 1665–1963* (Scottish Record Society, 1990), 72, 109.

4. *Cambridge University: St John's College Admissions*, part 3 1715–67 (1903), 129, 590. *Victoria County History of Cambridgeshire*, vi (1978), 168, 175.

5. Nichols, John, *Literary Anecdotes of the Eighteenth Century*, iv (1812), 665; Horsfield, *op. cit.*, ii, 250; *Dictionary of National Biography* entries for John Taylor and Andrew Ducarel. The date given in *DNB* for Burrell's admission to the Society of Antiquaries of London is incorrect.

6. *Dictionary of National Biography* entries for Samuel Gale and Andrew Ducarel.

7. [Kemp, D. W., ed.], *Tours in Scotland, 1747, 1750, 1760 by Richard Pococke* – (Scottish History Society, 1887), xliv–xlvi, lviii, lxi.

8. *The Record of Old Westminsters*, i (1928), 483.

9. Kemp, *op. cit.*, 355.

10. [Morris, Christopher, ed.], *The Journeys of Celia Fiennes* (1967), xxxii.

11. The reference to Gordon's account of the Aberlemno stones takes the form of a marginal gloss (p. 108, fol. 31^r).
12. Tait, A. A., *The Landscape Garden in Scotland 1735–1835* (1980), 33–6, 52–5.
13. Cited in *Scottish Architects at Home and Abroad*, National Library of Scotland (1978), 25–6.
14. This practice, which was not confined to the Highlands, had long excited the curiosity of travellers to Scotland. See [Brown, P. Hume, ed.], *Early Travellers in Scotland* (1891), 143 and index.
15. Mitchell, Arthur, *List of Travels and Tours in Scotland 1296 to 1900* (1902), 504–528 (reprinted from *Proceedings of the Society of Antiquaries of Scotland*, xxxv (1900–1). Bishop Pococke made short expeditions into Scotland in 1747 and 1750, but his main tour was not undertaken until 1760.

The Journal

I set out from London Saturday July 8th on a tour into the north of Scotland and travelled post that night to Baldock 37 miles from London, the weather being very bad so that I had neither time nor opportunity of making such observations in my journey as either my own genius or a desire to execute your injunctions prompted me to. The lands in the neighbourhood of Baldock in general are poor and let at an average from 4 to 5 shillings per acre and sell at 22 years' purchase. Their produce is chiefly wheat and barley; the latter meets with the most encouragement. The sole trade of this and the neighbouring towns consists in malting, which in this is conveyed by land to Ware and thence by water to London.

From thence I crossed a deep and bad country 8 miles to Royston on the 9th [July], to which place the lands are much of the same sort and value, except when you come close to the town, where the price is increased, but they are reduced to their real value within the distance of a mile. At Royston are 34 malt kilns, a manufacture of wyre for the kilns, another for weaving sacking cloth for ditto, both very considerable. The cave[1] is 80 feet deep under the market house and 30 feet diameter; many rude figures carved on the wall, on which *vide* Dr Stukely's bold conjectures. Royston parish does not extend one foot beyond the site of the town; its only trade is malt.

From thence at the distance of 3 miles stands Wimple < Wimpole >, the seat of Lord Hardwick. It has an avenue of trees to the house about a mile in length, which comes down to the roadside, for grandeur only, not use. The way to the house is about 2 miles north, close to the Tyger alehouse, where a key is left, but under such restrictions that it cannot be lent to any person that is not intimately connected with the owner, and I not having that honour was not permitted to see it. From the little observation I was able to make, one part of the park appears greatly indebted to nature for beauties, which have received no advantage from art or expence. It is a very pleasant hill, commanding an extensive prospect on every side. Upon the whole it appears to a traveller to savour more of oeconomy than nobility.

From hence I went to Caxton, a small, vile, dirty post town 11 miles north of Royston, without any circumstance to recommend itself to travellers except the furnishing them with post horses to leave it. The houses, or rather huts, consist entirely of clay and denote thereby the poverty of its inhabitants. The farms hereabouts are from £50 to £200 per annum and are sowed with wheat, barley and oats, very few beans, no rye.

From hence to Huntingdon is 9 miles, the whole way open country with nothing to divert the attention of passengers, the prospects so dreary and extensive that they rather weary than please the eye, terminating generally in water. The grain here chiefly wheat and barley, few oats and no beans or peas; malt is the chief commodity. Here we rested, having met my friend Mr Symonds < the Rev. John Symonds, his travelling companion >.

Monday the 10th < July >. We set out for Stilton 12 miles distant, remarkable for nothing but their former good qualities of making a rich sort of cheese. On the road there are a few small enclosures very serviceable to the tenant, who takes in gist cattle < cattle taken in to feed >; the grain, wheat and barley. Close to Stilton is a small hop ground, the property of Mr Cowper Thornhill,[2] with this particularity that it is surrounded with willow trees to guard the hops against the violence of the wind. It is most exposed to the north west. The country hereabouts is deep (if you go off the turnpike road, which is very fine); it is not far from the fens. The mud walled cottages indicate the poverty of the inhabitants. The lands belong chiefly to Sir John Heathcote. The price of labour is from 8d to 10d per day. Provisions are cheap. To Stamford is 14 miles. At Chesterton, about 4 miles from Stilton, are to be seen some fine inclosures divided into from 20 to 30 acres, situated on a descent, the hedgerows planted with good trees on every side; the inclosures chiefly grazing lands and turn to good account. This estate belongs to a Pigot < ?Robert Pigott > of Shropshire. Near Stamford some lands of Lord Exeter's are inclosed in a very extraordinary and expensive manner. A row of quick is planted between hurdles on one side and post and rails on the other.

At Wandsford you exchange the clay huts of Huntingdonshire for houses of Northamptonshire stone more pleasing to the eye and advantageous to the inhabitant. They are built without cement; at least in the poor cottages none appears on the outside. The noble palace at Burghley is too fine to be described; I shall only say it was the work of the great Burghley. There is a great number of good pictures by eminent masters, particularly Rubens, Carlo Dolce, Carlo Maratt and the two Poussins, not to forget the famous *Seneca Dying in the Bath* by L[uca] Jordano. The jewel closet is filled with curiosities and precious stones to a great value. It is much improved by the present lord, who has new roofed the house and intends to fit up the great hall, staircase and 4 magnificent rooms which have never been floored or furnished, though the walls and cieling have been adorned at great expence by Verrio and Laguerre. The park is full of trees, not profitable but ornamental, which are very pleasing to the eye. Stamford is a very neat town built of the country stone, which has a good effect and it is as difficult here to meet with a bad house as a good one is in Huntingdonshire.

Tuesday July 11. We made an excursion to Grimsthorp, the seat of the Duke of Ancaster, and about 3 miles from Stamford passed by Royal < Ryhall >, a village belonging to Mr Burrell, very pleasantly situated, commanding the best prospect of Burleigh Park. The way to Grimsthorp is extremely pleasant, especially the 2 last miles, which consists of meadows full of risings and swellings with trees interspersed amongst them. The park itself is the finest I ever saw. You are conducted through an avenue 3 miles long, at the end of which the house presents itself to your view situated on a high hill before which is a noble lawn and in the bottom a serpentine river, on one side of which are many gentle risings cloathed with hanging woods.

From hence to Coltsworth <Colsterworth> is 8 miles. In our passage thither we passed Corbet <Corby> Common (a Grimsthorp in miniature). We rode at the bottom of 2 little hills remarkable for their fine verdure and the young woods that flanked them on each side. From Coltsworth to Belvoir Castle is 11 miles mostly cross road, difficult to find. The castle is visible at a great distance, being situated on a prodigious eminence and commanding the most extensive prospect on every side. But were it not to be seen, the badness of the roads would sufficiently indicate they lead to Belvoir. The height of situation renders it much exposed to the violence of north winds which sometimes destroy whole sashes. The apartments are large, but not well fitted up. It is stripped of most of the capital pictures, which are carried to Knightsbridge, and amongst them the famous *Drunken Sea Monster*. The road to Grantham is bad, but that is in some small degree made up to a traveller by many agreable views which present themselves to his sight. It is about 7 miles distant. The lands in the Vale of Belvoir continue at the old rents and are let on an average at £0 2s 6d per acre; the present duke and his son, Lord Granby, are unwilling to raise them. There is no park, but the wild deer lye all round the vale. The price of labour is about £0 1s 0d in harvest; at other times from 6d to 8d per day. Grantham has nothing to boast of but its neatness, no manufacture being carried on there.

Wednesday 12th <July>. From hence to Belton, Lady Cust's, is a mile through a long sandy lane. There is a good avenue of trees before the house; within nothing worth seeing but the library which is beautyfull and curious. The waterwork, or rather cascade, is pretty but not capital. In our way to Ancaster, at Hunnington <Honington>, we were greatly sur-prized with the sight of a mill for grinding woad, the process of which is as follows. They first grind it to a jelly, then make it into round balls (the size of mustard balls) and lay it on hurdles to dry. When dry they put it into pens in heaps, then grind them to a powder again and wet them every day for 7 or 8 weeks together, at the end of which it is rammed into hogsheads of 1500 pounds weight each and sent thence to the dyers. The soil on which this woad grows is a reddish sand and clay mixed. The people employed in gathering it perform their part on their knees with spuds without handles and cut it with surprizing dexterity; it yields 3 crops in a year. The lands thus planted near Marnham let at £3 15s 0d the first year, £3 10s 0d the 2nd per acre, then the tenant gets a crop of corn off it at the usual rent and then it is laid down with seeds. The tenant to find the seed if he gets 2 crops of corn; if but one, the landlord.

Ancaster is 7 miles from Grantham, a dirty, paultry village unworthy notice. Thence to Lincoln is 20 miles over a long heath the greatest part of the way, on one side of which you discover now and then a village. But the prospect on the right is terminated by no very pleasing prospect, the fens at Lincoln. Provisions are dear; the price of labour is £0 1s 0d in summer, from 6d to 8d in winter. The size of the farms in general are about £100 per annum. The plough land lets at an average at £0 15s 0d per acre, the meadow at £1 0s 0d. The cathedral is remarkably beautyfull and noble, but greatly decayed and out of repairs. At the chaunter's house is a Roman hypocaust to which you descend a pair of damp stairs under ground about 10 foot and then if curiosity prompts you to proceed it must be on hands and knees at the expence of your cloathes. The Roman gate, castle keep and assembly room have each their respective beautyes.

To Spittle in the Street is 12 miles across the heath. On the right hand you have a pleasant but distant view of the woulds of Lincolnshire; the left affords a dreary prospect without any one new object to releive the eye except Lord Scarborough's dog kennel <?Glentworth Hall>, which may possibly afford entertainment to a foxhunting squire, but had not that effect on me or my companion. Here ends the beautyfull Roman road which appears first near Ancaster and is continued in a straight line to Spittle.

From thence 11 miles dirty road brings you to Glamford Bridges, or as it is styled by the country people, Bridge and Brig. It is situated on the River Anculm <Ancholme>, which branches from and returns into the Humber. It is navigable for one masted vessels and carries on a good traffick in corn and wool with the neighbouring county of York and brings back in return grocery, mercery, coals and coke, or cinders, in abundance for drying malt, great quantities of which is dryed here. It is well situated for the woolen trade; provisions are tolerably cheap. The prices of labour is in winter from 6 to 8 pence per day, in summer 14 pence. The farms are from £10 to £500 pounds per annum; plough land lets from 6 pence to £0 2s 6d per acre, meadow from £0 5s 0d to £1 5s 0d per acre. In general the land tax is easy, particularly amongst the gentlemen. Mr Pelham of Broclesby (the monarch of this part of the country) don't pay £0 1s 6d when the land tax is £0 4s 0d in the pound.

All sorts of grain grows here and large quantities of hemp and flax. A great extent of land that is now unprofitable might be made fit for cultivation at a very small expence if the owners would agree about the manner of doing it, for want of which 22,000 acres remain fenny and useless, which may easily be drained and the water carried off into the Humber. The soils are as various as the prices the lands let at, consisting of clay and different sorts of sand. There is also a great deal of land where there is not 4 inches soil before you come to the calk stone. They manure the land with dung, soot, pigeon muck (but this must be done with great skill and caution and at proper seasons of the year only and care must be taken that the land on which it is laid is such as will not suffer from the heat of it), malt combs and lime; the last of these is used chiefly on sandy lands. Mr Pelham buys in many small farms and consolidates them into one great farm which, whilst is serviceable to the landlord and tenant, hath one bad effect, that of depopulating the country.

To the ferry house at Barton is 11¾ miles. The way thither is much the same as on the Lincoln side, little else being visible than a barren heath till you come to Mr Thompson's enclosures, who has planted some part of the road above his house with clumps of evergreens and forest trees mixed, and above these at < blank > the same sort of trees on each side, which produces a very good effect. Barton is a dirty village ½ a mile from the banks of the Humber. It has neither trade nor manufactures. The arable land here lets at 4 shillings per acre, though it is good. The reason is that an acre here is not above ¾ of an acre and there is very little common land or inclosures. The whole grazing land of the parish does not exceed 200 acres and that will let at 40 shillings per acre. There is one corn field here, the largest in England, it consists of 6000 acres, so that here is a great quantity of corn, few sheep. There are no headlands or baulks throughout this whole field to distinguish one person's property from another, yet the farmers are so exact that each man knows his own extent and it very seldom happens that any one incroaches on his neighbour. The harvest is done by the acre, on which account they are extremely quick and often do 2 days' work in one. Provisions are cheap, the land tax easy, soil good, manure only dung. When going to sow they sometimes steep the grain in salt water, sometimes lime it, to prevent mildew. The land sells at 30 years' purchase.

From Barton to Hull the passage by water is about 6 miles. The usual passage is about an hour if the wind is fair; we passed it in ¾ of an hour, the wind blowing fresh and standing as fair as possible. At this ferry there is the best accomodation boat I ever saw and it is remarkable that no boat was ever lost in this passage.

Hull is a large town, the streets narrow and the houses not good. It carries on a large trade in woolen goods to almost all parts of Europe and America from the West Riding of York, whose carrier it may be fairly styled. There are 300 sail of ships belonging to this port. This place is capable of being made extremely strong (as it appeared in the civil wars). They can lay the country under water 5 miles round the town and the adjacent parts are so low and level that it cannot be commanded from any part so as to do any material or essential damage. In the time of Charles the First, when the king's army lay before it, a battery erected close by Sutton windmill destroyed a few houses and part of one of the gates, but proceeded no farther in their design. The castle, or garrison, as it is now christened, is little more than a heap of ruins and serves only to shew its pristine strength. It has a governor and a garrison of 100 invalids. The first enjoys thereby a good sinecure and you may judge of the utility of the latter by their mounting guard in summer in greatcoats.

The town is populous, the number of inhabitants amounts to 30,000 souls. Here is a very neat Trinity House formed into an oblong square; the foundation is for the widows of 32 sailors, who are allowed lodging, firing and £0 2s 6d per week in money. They have a chapel wherein prayers is read 3 times a week and a sermon once in a quarter of a year. At Hull Heswell Gate, where Charles the First summoned Sir John Hotham, is shut up and never used as a thoroughfare. Provisions are cheaper here than in any place in Yorkshire. The price of labor is for shipping £0 2s 0d per day; in harvest, men £0 1s 2d, women £0 0s 8d per day. Men in winter £0 1s 0d from 6 in morning to 6 in evening. It is usual for the men to thrash in winter for 4 and 5 pence per day and victuals. Meadow and plowed land are here usually let together at £0 6s 6d per acre, though some meadow land within a mile of the town is let from £3 10s 0d to £5 0s 0d per acre. All sorts of corn is sowed here, nothing else. The farms run from £20 to £300 per annum. The manure is dung and soap ashes. The soil is sand and strong clay, generally the latter. 10 miles further a light sand generally prevails. The land tax is very easy, not amounting to 12 pence in the pound when the land tax is at £0 4s 0d in the pound, the man at the Black Bull and Swan paying only 30 shillings for £40 per annum. At Hull the women wear an odd kind of straw bonnet which makes them appear extremely frightfull.

From Hull to Beverley is 9 miles, the greatest part of the way a dead flat, the rest small enclosures. Beverley itself is a neat town, well built for the greatest part. The minster is a most beautyfull Gothick building worthy the attention of every traveller. The inside is fitted up most magnificently; the carved work over the stalls in the choir is of Irish oak, which has this peculiar felicity that spiders will not harbour there. The altar is the neatest I ever saw. There is left £600 per annum for the repair of this minster, which is kept in the neatest manner. But the managers of this fund have erred strangely in the application of it, for they have filled up the small isles, or rather that part of them adjoining to the choir, with pews on each side for the general performance of service, reserving the choir only for the communion service, which however well intended by them hath this bad effect, that it spoils the look of the church. On the south side of the cross isle is King Athelstan's grant of immunity from payment of toll in any port of England to the inhabitants of Beverley in these words: *Als free make I thee as heart can wish or eye can see.* There is the picture of St John and Athelstane with the grant in his hand.

Here is a noble house belonging to Sir Charles Hotham, but not inhabited by him at present, he being averse to *rus in urbe.* I had almost forgot to mention the cupola,[3] which the stupidity, not the ingenuity, of man placed there; it has a very bad effect. For my own part I am at a great loss to account for so gross an absurdity being committed and think it would not be more ridiculous to cloath Cato the censor in Harlequin's coat, or that of a modern fine gentleman, than to join a modern cupola to a Gothick building. Upon a close examination I have since learnt that it was only placed there to preserve the tower till a steeple or spire can be built in its place.

There is no manufacture, plenty of fish and all sorts of provisions as cheap as in any part of Yorkshire. No church rates for either church, each being endowed with lands sufficient for the repairs. Poor's rate amounts to 12 pence in the pound. Round the town are a great number of inclosures and the lands are good. The soil is gravel and clay, mostly the latter. 4 large commons or pastures on which every freeman is entitled to keep 16 head of cattle all the summer, paying 30 shillings towards repairing the dykes and hedges and the people that take care of them. Lands in this country are not let by the acre, but by a measure called an uskin < oxgang >, containing nine acres. Nor do they distinguish between meadow and arable, but let them together at £5 per uskin, which is equal to 11 shillings 1 penny per acre and (3 pence over). The land tax here is 9 pence in the pound, or £0 15s 0d for £20, now the tax is at £0 4s 0d. The price of land is 35 years' purchase; farms < run > from £30 to £100 per annum. Labour in Beverley is £0 1s 3d per day; in the neighbourhood from 8 to 10 pence in summer and 4 pence in winter. Manure, dung. At Hull and Beverley more pretty girls than from London to the Humberside.

Saturday 15th < July >. The weather being extremely bad we were obliged to travel in a post chaise from Beverley to York, 32 miles without having any objects to look at but barren commons and black moors till we were within 2 miles of the northern capital, where stands a pretty house belonging to Colonel Cundum < ?Duncombe >, a name of reputation in these parts.

The chief things of note at York is first the cathedral, which is a noble fabrick and is kept with the greatest neatness and exactness. The windows of this church are all remarkably beautyfull and well preserved; the east window in particular is esteemed the most curious in Great Britain. The roof is clean, not fine, and greatly inferior in this respect to that at Lincoln. The choir is elegantly fitted up, but appears too narrow for its length. The chapterhouse has likewise its excellencies, being built in such a manner as to require no pillar in the middle for the support of the roof. There are several curiosities shewn in the vestry, as Ulphus's horn, several rings belonging to the diocesans, some so old as the 12th century, likewise the tops of croziers of the same date and being taken out of the same coffins. There is one silver crozier, about 5 feet, remarkable only on this account, that when James 2nd on a vacancy sent down a papist to fill the see of York, as he was making his public entry into the cathedral the gentlemen of the county attacked him and took away his crozier, which has been preserved there ever since as a testimony to shew that tyranny and superstition, though enjoined by the commands of the sovereign, will not be tamely submitted to by those who are educated in the true principles of liberty.

The next thing that demanded our attention was the castle, or prison, which for beauty, neatness and convenience exceeds any other in the kingdom. At Micklegate Bar is a Roman arch of the Tuscan order compleat and well preserved. On the wall of the churchyard of St Lawrence extra Walmgate 2 old statues lye prostrate whether R[oman] or S[axon] is uncertain; many coins and urns have been found there. The remains of St Mary's Abbey, or as it is now called, the manor, is worth seeing; it is a girls' boarding school. Old Baile, or Bishopshill, commands a good view both of the town and river; it is planted with trees. Ouse bridge, the middle arch 81 feet wide from the first spring of the arch and 17 feet high, formerly esteemed one of the largest in Europe, probably built in 1235. Clifford's Tower, now in an attorney's garden, close to the gaol.

In York, St Martin's parish, the poor's rate £0 1s 2d in the pound; a poor house in every parish. The land tax is £0 1s 6d when by Act of Parliament at £0 4s 0d. Land sells here at 35 years' purchase. Labor in summer is men from 8d to 1s, women 4d to 6d per day. Winter, men from 6d to 8d, women washing 6d and victuals. Farms are from £10 to £100 per annum. Manure, marl, dung and much lime in corn land; much grass land here. Provisions dear; mutton 4d per pound. 35,000 inhabitants. Trade, iron and deal from Hamburgh. Here was brought me a stem of oats 5 feet 10 inches high, had 34 branches, was the thickness of my little finger. It was taken out of a field belonging to Mr Bond, a noted horse dealer and farmer in York, who said the whole field had as large stems, some few much larger. I had almost omitted to mention the noble assembly room, which is 120 ft long, 40 ft wide, 40 ft high. It consists of 18 pillars on each side and 4 at each end; 17 windows on each side and 5 at each end. It is so magnificent that it is an honor to the county of York. The seats are gilt and covered with crimson damask and so contrived that the dancers are not liable to be interrupted by those who set by.

Monday 17th <July>. We set out for Helmsley, Mr Duncomb's, 25 miles distant from York, the roads to it extremely bad and to add to our misfortune it rained the whole day. In our way thither we passed by an old battered seat <Gilling Castle> of the Irish Lord Fairfax (a papist). The village near it indicated the utmost poverty. The place is capable of great improvements, nature having contributed largely in the disposition of hill and vale agreably interspersed, the former covered with woods for 2 or 3 miles.

Duncomb Park was formerly the seat of the Duke of Buckingham mentioned by Pope for his extravagence and the poverty in which he died. He sold the seat and estate of £6000 per annum to a Duncomb. It is now improved to £9000 per annum and was at that time of day esteemed the largest purchase in England. The old house is pulled down and a new one erected with one wing, the other wing not yet begun. The gardens are extremely beautyful, particularly the terraces a ¼ of a mile in length, at one end of which is a temple of Vesta, the other of < blank >. The descent from it is remarkably steep and fringed with wood from the top to the bottom, where is a small river very subject to floods after severe rains, which sometimes are so violent as to carry away every thing that opposes its passage, for which reason the kitchen garden is to be removed.

The opposite hill is equally steep and cloathed with noble woods. 2 miles distant from the house is another terrace ½ a mile long; at one end is a round temple, at the other a square ditto containing a room 27 by 18 feet, the architrave, freeze and cornice elegantly carved and gilt; the cieling is well painted by Berners < Giovanni Borgnis >, an Italian, on which is represented the *Aurora* of Guido. Below is a kitchen, bedchamber, cellar with all conveniences for dineing there. This terrace commands a fine view of the spatious ruins of Rivolx Abbey, situated in the vale immediately below and within 2 miles the race ground of Black Hambleton. The beauties are greatly heightened by the extensive moors and bad country that surround it.

Meadow and arable lands let for £0 15s 0d to £1 10 0d per acre, sells at 35 years' purchase. Manure, dung and lime. Method of cultivation is as follows. They lime the land for wheat with the sowing down. After plowing, a crop of oats for first sowing, a crop of barley to succeed, then a fallow, and then wheat with lime. Labor in summer, for men 10d, women 5d per day; haying 6d. Winter, men if not constant 10d, if constant 8d throughout the year. Farms < run > from £10 to £100 per annum. Poor rates £0 2s 0d in the pound. Provisions very dear in respect of labor. Wheat £0 5s 0d per bushel, beef and mutton £0 0s 3d per pound.

Helmsly is a market town. To New Malton is 18 computed miles (the roads and weather extremely bad). It is situate on the River Darwent and is navigable for small coal vessels. It falls into the Ouze 20 miles below York and then emptyes itself into the Humber. The town is neat, has no manufacture; provisions dear, coals £0 16s 0d per chaldron, which is reckoned dear, the reason of which is the river is farmed at £700 per annum. There are several locks; for passing through them the tenant obliges the boats to pay a large fee. The coals are brought from Leeds and Wakefield. The country hereabouts plentyfull. The land tax now at £0 4s 0d, they pay £0 0s 9d in the pound. The poor rates £0 1s 0d. Farms <run> from £15 to £200 per annum. Manure, lime and dung. Labor, men in summer £0 1s 0d, women 5d and 6d per day; winter, men £0 0s 10d . Land, 40 years' purchase. Mutton and beef 4d per pound. Arable land lets at £0 10s 0d, meadow at £1 0s 0d per acre.

Hence to Castle Howard and back to Malton is 10 miles, bad road. The house, or rather palace, is a truly noble and magnificent aedifice, built after Sir John Vanbrugh's plan and the lightest of that sort that I ever saw. There are a great number of large rooms filled with some good pictures; the works of Panini and Canaletti are the most in number. There are here a great number of antique busts and inscriptions, which see at the end of this book,[4] some few antique medallions, statues and vases, but in variety of antique marbles disposed in tables exceeds any place in England.

In the park is a beautyfull mausoleum for the remains of the Carlisle family, which cost £17,000. The upper part is a chappel, elegantly fitted up, the pavement mosaic work. Below is several apartments divided into 4 separate outlets containing several columbaria, or holes, each big enough for the reception of one body, as is likewise the circle in which the building is formed big enough in the whole to contain 63 bodies. The park is most agreably disposed, being flanked on all sides with woods interspersed with temples, statues, obelisks and a pyramid.

From Malton to Scarborough is 23 miles, tolerable turnpike road. In the way you see a seat of Sir William St Quintin <Scampston>, who has planted clumps of fir trees in the front and on each side the house for the space of 2 miles, which produces a most surprising effect and shews what art and expence is capable of doing in beautyfying the most barren and disagreable country. Farther is a small seat belonging to Mr Thompson <?Settrington> on the side of a hill covered with woods, which is remarkably pretty.

Scarborough is pleasantly situated at the bottom of a bay commanding an excellent view of the sea. It is well calculated for the coal trade, in which it employs, together with its coasting trade <blank> sail of ships. Farms here are from £4 to £50. Land sells at 30 years' purchase and lets in the country at £0 10s 0d per acre. Within a mile of the town meadow and pasture at £2 0s 0d, small closes adjoining to the town at £3 0s 0d per acre. Labor here £0 1s 0d per day all the year, or £0 0s 6d and victuals. Women for haying £0 0s 8d, a gill of ale and halfpenny roll. For throwing incle hills <inkle healds> £0 0s 6d and ditto. Manure, dung, lime and seaweed. Provisions very dear; wheat £0 5s 0d per bushel.

The castle is situated on a prodigious eminence commanding the sea every way. It is naturally extremely strong and was justly esteemed impregnable at the time it was built, before the use of guns was known. It is commanded from a hill on the opposite side of the town near the spa, where Cromwell erected a battery which did great execution. A Frenchman named Stafford, with a few of his countreymen, possessed themselves of it once and held out some days, but at last were obliged to capitulate. There is a small battery on the south descent, which commands the point for a mile and half and thereby prevents the too near approach of an enemy's privateers. Whilst I was there, a small one appeared within 4 or 5 miles of the shore, upon which the flag was hoisted as a signal for all ships to be on their guard and keep in close to the coast. The walls of this fortification are almost entire. There is the remains of the tower, destroyed in the civil wars. There was another to correspond with it till the late Duke of Montagu caused it to be pulled down and erected a brick building for barracks in the scite where it stood, which has a very bad appearance from the town. The barracks are good and there is a regular guard mounted; in garrison is a company of the train of artillery.

The coast is flat in the bay, the bottom a fine hard sand which renders it very convenient for bathing. Here much company repair for that purpose in the season, which begins the latter end of June and lasts till the end of August. Those who bath are drawn by a horse in a small covered waggon, fixed on 4 wheels of an equal size, to a proper depth, where they are conducted by a guide. When they have staid a sufficient time in the water they return to their waggons, where they dress themselves and then are conducted back. To this and the spa the town is indebted for great part of its support. Here is great plenty of good fish, particularly turbot, soles and whitings. From one of the publick rooms there is a good prospect of the bay, by which all ships that pass and repass may be seen to advantage. The spa is so close to the sea that at spring tides it is sometimes affected by the salt water.

From hence we crossed a barren moor to Hackness, a most beautyfull romantick situation greatly heightened by the disagreeable country that surrounds it. It is situated in a deep vale of great extent, environed with high hills on every side fringed with wood from top to bottom. In the midst of the vale runs a serpentine rivulet bordered by fertile meadows. Every step you go presents some new object equally striking and agreable. Between each hill you behold a beautyfull though small vale ornamented and enriched by nature, which have received no improvement by art; in short it looks like the Eden of Britain. From Hackness Head you command an extensive prospect of the sea. This lordship < Hackness > belongs to Lord Annandale, who has a house there inhabited only by a farmer. This estate formerly was in the possesson of Sir Thomas Hobby, from whom it passed to Sir Philip Sydenham and from him to the present owner.

From Scarborough to Whitby is 19 miles across one continued black moor, where in some places there is no roads to direct the traveller and where the guides of the country are often themselves mistaken. And to add to these disagreable circumstances, you seldom meet with even a shepherd to direct you. At Whitby Mr Cholmondly <Cholmley> has built a large house <Abbey House> close to Whitby Abbey. It is situated upon a high hill which might command a noble and extensive prospect (having the sea in front, on the other side Whitby river adorned with high banks covered with wood, and beyond a great range of cultivated country; at the foot of the hill is Whitby town) had not the stupidity of its owner contrived to shut out the view of the town by stables, dog kennels etc, the sea by high walls. The most pleasant room in the house is very judiciously converted to a kitchen. The abbey is a terrible prospect of the Gothick disposition of its former owner who, when he built the dwelling house, gutted this noble aedifice and it now stands almost subdued by time, the arches and roofing being entirely fallen in and the whole place, once the asylum of religion, is now become an habitation for rabbits.

The descent to the town of Whitby is the steepest I ever saw and on the other side you have a pleasant ride along the sands to Mr Phipps's allum work (when the tide is out). This manufacture is the largest in England and well worthy the inspection of the curious. The process of it is as follows. About a ¼ of a mile distant they dig the allum earth and lay it in a heap with different layers of furze and brushwood and burn it, then throw it into a pit into which water is let to steep it. When steeped, it is conveyed through troughs underground into the allum house into a large cistern, whence it runs into the pans. Boyled there 24 hours and run off into settlers, where it stands 2 or 3 hours till the slime settles to the bottom, then run off into coolers where it is mixed with urine. Stands in these 4 days, when the allum strikes from the liquor to the sides. It is then shaved off and carried into a bing, then thrown into a pan and boyled a 2nd time, then run into large casks and kept there a fortnight, then broke up. NB They steep the kelp or sea weed in water and mix it with the allum water. At Whitby they mend their roads with mould.

From Whitby to Mulgrave is 4 miles to Mr Phipps, who has a very pretty hunting seat <Mulgrave Castle> built by the Duke of Buckingham, but has received great improvements from the present owners, Mr Phipps and Lady Lepel. It is situated on the top of a hill about half a mile from the sea. On the back front is a spatious grass walk planted on each side with evergreens and ash trees, from which there is a beautyfull prospect of the sea. In front they look over a tolerable country entirely bare of wood, except a vale belonging to Mr Phipps with the hills on both sides of it, at the top of which is the ruins of <Old> Mulgrave Castle, now a heap of rubbish. At the bottom of the hills runs a small stream quite through the vale, which might be made extremely pretty, as well as the woods, if the absurdity of the country would permit it. But their claim of turning beasts into the woods to browze renders all intentions of the owner to beautify it ineffectual.

About 8 miles from Mulgrave stands a small fishing town called Stathes, which for its romantick situation is much to be admired. It is close to the sea in a small bay surrounded with hills remarkably high, is extremely populous and carryes on a large trade in salt fish, particularly cod and old maids <bivalve molluscs>. From Mulgrave to Gisborough is 15 miles over a wild moor. Here I expected to entertain myself with the large ruins of an abbey <Guisborough Priory> mentioned by Camden <*Britannia* (1695), 353> as remarkably fine, but found the interval between the time of Elizabeth and George 2nd had caused great alteration, there being nothing remaining but a great window, which indeed wore a noble aspect. The village is clean and well built.

Hence to Stockton in the bishoprick of Durham is 12 miles to the Tees side, where we ferryed over. It is a good market town consisting of 1 street very broad and well built. Here is a manufacture of sail cloth and a good trade in corn, lead, butter and pork to Norway, Sweden and Russia, from whence they bring back deal, iron and flax. Land here sells for 35 years' purchase. There is little arable, which lets at £0 15s 0d per acre; meadow ditto from £1 0s 0d to £3 0s 0d per acre. Farms run from £8 0s 0d to £120 0s 0d per annum. Manure, kelp and dung mixed. Labour, men in summer per day for mowing £0 2s 0d, women haying £0 0s 6d and beer; men in winter £0 0s 10d. Provisions reasonable. Poor rates £0 1s 6d on land and stock; houses £0 1s 0d in the pound.

To Sedgefield is 10 miles, where is a good market for butcher's meat on Fridays. Labour in summer, men £0 0s 10, women £0 0s 8. Winter, men £0 0s 6d, women £0 0s 4d per day. Farms from £5 0s 0d to £200 0s 0d per annum. Meadow lets from £0 5s 0d to £1 10s 0d per acre. Manure only dung. Soil, gravel, clay and sand. Mutton sells at 3½d, beef at 4d per pound. Wheat at £0 4s 6d to £0 5s 6d per boll. At Hardwick <Hall>, ¼ of a mile from hence, are some gardens belonging to Mr Burdon, very extensive and judiciously laid out. There is 1 piece of water in them 36 acres, and a pretty serpentine river not yet compleated.

10 miles more brought us to Durham. The approach to it is very magnificent. It is situated on a hill, the sides of which towards Sedgfield are covered with wood, chiefly oak, and at the bottom of the vale runs a tolerable stream. The cathedral has little to recommend it but its antiquity. The pillars are unsightly and disagreable. The carved work in the choir is good and the skreen at the altar is esteemed a work of merit. It is of the same order of architecture with the church, which in other cathedrals is seldom observed. In the library is a good collection of books, chiefly religious though there are some classicks and several manuscripts, particularly of Plato. There are many stones with inscriptions taken from the Picts' Wall, published in Horsley <*Britannica Romana* (1732)>. The bishop's palace is a large old building, formerly a place of

strength. There is now an octagon tower which is called the castle, but it is stopped up and is now only a memorial of its pristine grandeur. The town is surrounded by the River Weare, the banks of which are formed into very pleasant walks covered with wood.

From Durham I passed to Rainton, a village where Lord Strathmore has a house. It is 4 miles from Durham. Thence we went to Fenkly <Finchale> Abbey, Houghton le Spring, Cocken and Hetton. The ruins of Fenkly Abbey are large and tolerably perfect. It is situated on the banks of a small river covered with wood on the opposite, which bears a small analogy to the Wye near Chepstowe. Here Mr Carr, the owner of Cocken, has cut a walk on the bank of the river, which has a good effect. From Rainton to Chester on the Street is 5 miles. In the way I saw Lumley Castle, esteemed one of the finest places in the north. It is well situated and commands the prospect of a good country. The woods that surround it are remarkably fine, but it is too much crouded with avenues which hide the prospect of a noble stream which runs very near, and might easily be seen from the house. There are on each side a grove of fur trees. The inside of the castle is truly noble, particularly the hall, dining room and the suite of rooms which the present owner has fitted up with crimson damask. The dining room is the largest I ever saw. It is fitted up with stucco, highly ornamented. The hall is filled with the pictures of the Lumley family from the conquest to the present time. Though the present possessor is seldom there, I must do him the justice to say I have not seen any large house in such good repair.

From Chester le Street to Gibbeside is 10 miles; it is the seat of Mr Bowes. The approach to the house is by a serpentine road covered on each side with great variety of evergreens and fruit trees. There are several vistos cut through the vale which affords a delightfull prospect; one of these presents to view an obelisk of the Doric order 144 ft high. At the top stands a statue of Liberty 12 ft 2 in high. It is well executed and has a good effect. It cost £2000 exclusive of the stone, which came from Mr Bowes's quarry. There is a banquetting house elegantly fitted up, a cold bath and other small seats. Farms run from £20 to £180 per annum. Meadow land lets from £0 10s 0d to £4 0s 0d per acre; arable from £0 10s 0d to £1 10s 0d. Manure, dung and lime mixed. Labor in summer is 10d men, 9d women per day. Soil gravel and loomy sand below. Provisions dear. Beef £0 0s 4½d per pound.

To Swallwell is 2½ miles; it is a dirty, nasty village. There is here a forge for making anchors. 4 miles further across the Tine stands Newborne <Newburn>; the way thither is extremely bad. It is a poor village of no note. 6 miles off is Harlow Hill, another inconsiderable town, where we lay at a very indifferent house. The master of it by his behaviour gave us no favorable impression of Northumbrian honesty, having made our servants pay a 2nd time for what we had before been charged. In our way thither at the 6 milestone from Newcastle we entred on the military road from Newcastle to Carlisle, one of the finest for the length and goodness of it in England. It is made on the Roman Wall, a bit of which we saw near Harlow about 2 yards in length with 5 rows of stone in height, and a little farther on a square stone 3 feet high with an inscription too much obliterated to make out.

Thence to Bramton is 35½ miles over a forlorn country without the appearance of a single tree till you come to Norworth <Naworth> Castle, the property of Lord Carlisle, who has made several plantations round the house and trees on each side of the road for a mile, which produce a good effect. It were to be hoped this beginning to improve that wild country may be followed by the inhabitants in those parts, as it will be both profitable and ornamental.

Carlisle is 9½ miles farther on. The road is much more agreable, particularly the entrance to the town, which is remarkably pretty (we passed 2 bridges built over 2 rivers, the Eden and Canda <?Caldew>); on each side is a vale of good meadows. There is little to be seen at Carlisle except the castle and abbey. The former was built by William Rufus and might possibly be esteemed a place of strength before the use of guns and batteries were invented. The situation of it will disprove any argument in favor of that now, being commanded from Stanwix Bank and several other places. The opinion of the government with respect to that point is evident from their permitting it to go to decay. At present there are 3 batteries to the west, 2 of 5 guns each and 1 of 3. On the northeast is a rampart with 10 large guns, the embrasures partly masonry, partly turf; the latter is daily mouldering away. The town is compleatly walled, but in one place close to the castle there is a breach wide enough for 6 men to enter abreast. I saw 3 pieces of canon in the castle, fit for use, lyeing neglected on the ground without carriages. Upon enquiry I was told representations had been made to the Board upon this and several other heads without effect and the same person added that those guns would in a short time be rendered unfit for service. The abbey is a meer old barn equally unsightly within and without.

I made an excursion during my stay here to Corbey, Mr Howard's seat (a Roman Catholic gentleman nearly related to Lord Carlisle). It is an old house situated on a high hill, at the foot whereof runs the rapid River Eden. The hill has not above 3 inches of soil before you come to the solid rock. It is lined with wood to the water edge and it is curious and surprising to see large oaks hanging from the top of the hill, whose roots have insinuated themselves so strongly into the stone that they have resisted the violence of winds which have destroyed trees not so much exposed. There is a good walk along the side of the hill, planted on each side. The sight and murmur of the water through the trees is extremely agreable. Meadow at Corbey from £0 15 0ds to £1 15 0d; arable from £0 12 0d to £1 8s 0d. Land sells at 30 years' purchase. Farms from £20 to £300. Provision cheap. Barley 6s per Carlisle bushel, which is equal to a Winchester bushel. Oats £0 5s 6d, wheat £0 15s 0d

Drumlanrig
Castle, Dumfries-
shire. Engraved
view after drawing
by Francis Grose,
c.1789.
(Reproduced by per-
mission of the
Royal Commission
on the Ancient and
Historical Monu-
ments of Scotland
(RCAHMS))

to £0 16s 0d, rye £0 10s 0d to £0 11s 0d, beans £0 8s 0d. Constant labourers 9d per day through the year, others 6d and victuals; women 6d. Mowing hay 14d per day and drink. Reaping oats 8d and 9d per day. Wheat ditto. Manure, lime, marl and dung.

From Carlisle to Annan is 18 miles. In our way we forded the Rivers Esk and < blank > < Sark >; the latter divides England and Scotland. As soon as I passed this, the first village produced a strong mark of the poverty of its inhabitants. The houses were built entirely of mud, without chimneys or windows, unless holes in the wall deserve that appelation. The inhabitants scorn the confinement of shoes and stockings and therefore go without either. They are averse to chimneys to discharge the smoak of their peet fires, because the passage of it through the door, they say, makes their huts warm. In some of these miserable cots there were windows, not casements but sashes, half of which were glass, the other wood. At a house belonging to Mr Blair at Annan I saw in the garden a stone fixed to the wall with this inscription:[5] *+ROBERT DE BRVS/ COVNTE DE GAL/RRIS ET SENT V D/DVAD DE/ ADD 1300/.*

From Annan to Dumfries is 18 miles, good road, the lands generally cultivated and produce flax, barley, wheat, oats and potatoes. Dumfries is a very neat town, has 2 churches and 3 tolerable inns. The King's Arms is the best in Scotland, kept by Mr McKune, a very civil man, the accomodation good. To Drumlangrig and back to Dumfries is 36 miles on the banks of the River Nith (on which Dumfries stands), the country well cultivated and produces, besides the grain above mentioned, buck wheat and hay. The Duke of Queensberry's house was built about 90 years ago of the stone of the country. The colour of it is red and disagreable to the eyes; they have whitewashed 3 sides of it in order to render it a more apparent object at a distance. The plantations are very noble and extensive, consisting of 700 acres. It is placed on an eminence, the less observable as it is surrounded on every side with prodigious mountains (though at some distance), and they barren, so that it may be truly said to resemble an equestrian statue placed in a barn. The land tax about Dumfries (when it is 4s) is from £0 1s 4d to £0 1s 6d. Manure is sea shells and sleech <deposited mud>. The gates to the fields in this neighbourhood bear a great resemblance to gibbets. The enclosures are walls of loose stones covered with mud, or mounds of earth sowed wth furze. In the inland parts the manure consists of marl and dung. Dumfries has a linen manufactory, rather for the environs than foreign consumption. Provisions are much the same price as at Carlisle.

From Dumfries to Newton Stewart is 54 miles. Little occurred by the way worthy observation, except an odd custom peculiar to that part of the country of bringing boyled eggs and Cheshire cheese to accompany the tea at breakfast. At another place I was forced to taste Scotch chicken broth bad enough to poison a Hottentot. The people have a method of styling all grounds enclosed parks, though perhaps some of these parks produce nothing for the benefit of man or beast. At Newton Stewart I was thrust into a vile room, remarkable for nothing but its dirt and the antiquity of its furniture. It was our dineing room and bedchamber and probably at other times performed the office of stable and hogstye conjointly. We were so fatigued that a strong desire of rest prompted us to lye down, but a stronger fear of the itch prevented us going into bed, so that we were obliged to trust to our own cloathes and even then were not without suspicion of an attack from the great beasts of these parts, in plain English, lice and fleas, the first remarkably large and violent in their proceedings. Fortunately we escaped these dangers, but were annoyed in the morning by a greater and more savage beast, the landlord, who cheated us most enormously.

To Glenluce is 14 miles over a horrid stony moor. It is a tolerable village situated on a hill above the bay of that name. 6 miles further is Stranraer, seated at the head of a spatious bay of the same name capable of containing 1000 sail of ships. It is landlocked on every side except the entrance, which is spatious yet not too wide, so that they might be protected from the violence of the wind on every side. In our way thither we went to Castle Kennedy, formerly belonging to Lord Stair, now to Mr Dalrymple. There are the ruins of the old castle standing, but the present owner is about to pull it down. It is most delightfully seated on a hill surrounded on every side by a loch of that name in which are several islands covered with wood, as indeed is the hill; and through the woods are cut several vistos to the water. It seems capable of being made one of the compleatest places in Great Brittain. Port Patrick is 6 miles more, a village remarkable for nothing but being the place of safest passage from Scotland to Ireland. It were pity the governement did not establish the packet regularly from that port as the conveyance is more quick and a safer passage than from Holyhead, the distance being only 10 leagues. At present, from the badness of the roads and accomodations, travellers chuse to go through Wales.

The packet boats are quite open, into which are men, women and children and all manner of beasts crouded promiscuously. The first village that presents itself on the Irish coast is called Donaghadee, almost as bad as Port Patrick. Here we landed between 12 and one Friday morning and having slept in our cloaths for 5 or 6 hours proceeded to Belfast, 18 miles distant. In our way thither I observed the enclosures were large; the fences were either stone walls, furze hedges or stones raised 2 feet and covered with mould. The crops are very fine, consisting of great quantities of grain, flax and potatoes. The meadows were almost everywhere overrun with docks and fern, a sad testimony of the negligence of the landholder. The country is good, the roads very fine, here and there interspersed with bogs, which the natives have given the name of dams and bearns, as being less obnoxious to the ear.

The entrance to Belfast is not pleasing, being through a horrid, long, stinking bog full of quicksands unpassable at high water; at low dangerous without a guide. Through it the women of the country walk composedly with their coats tucked up to their waists. Thence we were conducted to a long causeway and bridge into the town, esteemed the 3rd in Ireland. It is a place of great trade, having 9 linen manufactorys, which alone employ 4 ships of 70 tons burthen, each loading 70 tons of linen, each ton containing 2000 pound weight of linen, each piece 7 pounds weight. They import a great quantity of manufactured tobacco from England, some little from Scotland, a very small quantity of unmanufactured ditto. Export; beef, butter and linen to the W[est] I[ndies]. The returns are sugar, tobacco and rum, the 2 former by way of England. From Sweden, Pomerania and Norway all their deals and timber are imported. From Holland all garden seeds and some small quantity of flax, but most of the drest flax from Dantzick. Between 3000 and 4000 heads of ditto from America. From Sweden all iron and steel, amounting yearly to 100 tons. The trade to England for coals takes off all their ready money, taking no goods in return, which is a great detriment to this country. Commissions are frequently sent from Manchester to buy up coarse linnen yarn.

There are 2 sugar houses, 1 salt pan and another building upon a new principle, that the same fire may [boyle] the salt and burn a kiln of lime at the same time. It is objected to this that the salt is not so good, because the lime requires a slow fire, whereas salt requires sometimes a quick fire, at other times none, or at most a lukewarm heat. The method of making salt is as follows. Get rock salt and dissolve it in water. That water is conveyed into the pans and made into salt. When made, they fill it into baskets and set it on hur[d]ls to drain off the liquor, which is put again into the pan. They put from 4 to 6 tons of rock salt into the cistern, according to the number of pans that is going. When put into the pan, it will boyl and make salt in 5 hours' time; the pan must be skimmed 6 times.

Arable land lets hereabouts at from £1 10s 0d to £2 0s 0d,

meadow at £4 0s 0d per acre. Manure, marl, dung and sweepings of the streets, for which they pay 2d per load. Oats sell at 9s per hundredweight, wheat 8s 6d ditto, barley 4s ditto, potatoes 1s per bushel, flax 12s per stone. The cottages in this country differ little from those in Scotland, except that those which have any windows are seldom sashed, but have casements. The poor people are stockingless and shoeless, some without breeches and almost in a state of nature. Their poverty is great, which is surprizing considering the plenty they enjoy and can be accounted for on no other principle but idleness and an entire aversion to labor.

To Antrim is 12 computed or 18 measured miles, the roads turnpike through a pleasant country, mostly open with little timber. Arable lets at 20s, meadow £1 8s 0d per acre; sells at 23 years' purchase. Labor 6d per day and victuals in harvest, the rest of the summer and winter at 6d. Manure, dung. Beef, mutton, lamb and veal 2d per pound. Wheat £1 2s 6d per barrell, but not likely to be worth half that sum in 6 weeks. Oats £0 7s 0d per barrell. Farms are from £10 to £30 per annum.

Antrim is a long ill-built town. It gives name to the county, yet is not the county town. It sends members to parliament and is styled by the electors a free borough, though Lord Massareen has the chief interest. He has an old house < Antrim Castle > and large gardens at one end of the town, but the present lord being a minor they are much neglected. Here I saw that species of duck which are said to hang by each others legs on the water so as to appear like things inanimate, but qu[estion] the truth of this report; those I saw had a very different appearance. There are many papists in Antrim, as indeed all this part of the country flocks with them, so that the farther you advance the more numerous you find them, to the great detriment of cultivation, as they are idle, negligent and bigotted. I enquired much after the wolf dog, but could meet with none throughout my whole tour, though they are said to be bred in this part of the island.

Ballymony lies 20 miles further. In our way thither a mile from Antrim we passed by Shane's Castle, Mr O'Neil's. It is esteemed the most antient building in Ireland, being erected before our Savior's birth. It stands at the edge of a very large lake called Lough Neagh; it belongs to Lord Mazareen. The farther we advanced into this part of the country, the less civilized the people appeared. They have neither shoes, stockings or breeches, entire strangers to shirts. Idleness, poverty and misery reigns amongst them. The greatest part of the inhabitants are bigotted Papists and so averse to Protestants that the latter will not venture to come amongst them for fear of being destroyed. The land is extremely fertile, but the occupants give themselves little trouble in the cultivation of it, so that many 100 acres lye in a manner waste, the consequence of which is that the same sort of land which in other parts let at £1 10s 0d here brings in only £0 7s 6d per acre. They are so prone to thieving that when they want provisions they steal their neighbours' cattle without ceremony.

Near Ballymony is a bog of 2000 acres. This a tolerable well-built town, the inhabitants chiefly Scotch Protestants. I had little opportunity of making any enquiries here, only staying whilst I baited the horses. In this part they have a method of stacking peat in the neatest manner. I took notice of a singular Irish plantation here viz. a quick hedge in a stone wall. The bridges of this country are not so good as those of Scotland. The people are civil to strangers and willing to shew them all the civilities in their power, but so addicted to blundering that to hear them and refrain from laughing is difficult, to take notice of them very imprudent and dangerous.

From Ballymoney to the Gyant's Causeway and back again is 24 miles, the longest I ever went. But my trouble was amply rewarded by the view of that surprizing curiosity, which to pass over in silence would be unjust, to attempt to give it all due praise, presumption in me. For a proper description of it I must refer you to the writers on that subject and shall content myself with observing it is a sort of inclined plain composed of pillars of stone exactly round, fixed into each other. Some appear 4 or 5 feet, some 20 feet high; the uprights of some are convex, of others concave. The whole extends itself a great way into the sea. At a little distance from these, in a detached part of the cliff, appear several columns so disposed as to resemble an organ.

Having spent some time in contemplating this great curiosity, I returned to my quarters at Ballymoney and thence to Donaghadee, which is 66 miles. Here I must note that arable land lets from £0 16s 0d to £1 16s 0d, meadow from £1 16s 0d to £2 0s 0d, marl at £1 10s 0d per acre. Land sells at 20 years' purchase. Manure, marl, dung and seaweed. Oatmeal sells at £0 9s 0d, wheat £0 8s 6d, barley £0 4s 0d per hundredweight, potatoes £0 1s 0d per bushel, flax £0 12s 0d per stone. Labor 5d per day and 4 meals of victuals.

To Portpatrick is 30 miles amd 6 miles to Stranraer, from whence we went to Ballantry <Ballantrae> 18 miles. The way is agreable, being partly round the pleasant bay of Stranraer, at the end of which we ascended a very high hill called the Glake <?Carlock> and 2 miles further enter the vale of Glennop, the situation of which is agreable and romantic. It is surrounded on each side with mountains, the edges of which are skirted in some places with corn, in others covered with bushes. At one end a hill terminates the prospect, the other is open to Stranraer Bay. In the middle runs a rivulet, small in summer, but from appearances rapid and impetuous after rains, not endowed with the good qualities of the Nile, which when it overflows enriches the land, but on the contrary covers every part with large stones that the impetuosity of the current drives down from the hills and by that means renders the best lands barren and useless. About Ballantry heathland lets at £0 1s 0d, arable £0 17s 6d, meadow £0 15s 0d per acre and sells from 30 to 35 years' purchase. The manure is dung and seaweed. Barley, oats and beans sell here at £0 13s 4d per bushel.

New Dily <Dailly> lyes 18 miles further. In our journey thither we coasted within a mile of Girvan to a place called the Salt Pans and saw distinctly several seals sporting on the water close to the shore. Along this coast we met with a great quantity of eringo root. Here we saw a prodigious barren rock in the sea called Ailsa Hill, where are found great flocks of solan geese at certain seasons of the year. It is quite barren and uninhabited. Some people go thither in search of the geese and to destroy the seals, which are very numerous at the bottom of the rock. The method is to strike them unawares on the back of the head with a stick, and if they do not kill them with that blow they seldom have an opportunity of succeeding in a second, but retire out of the animal's reach to avoid danger.

At the Salt we left the sea and entered a very beautyfull vale through alder groves to Bargany, the seat of Mr Hamilton, whose house and garden are in the old taste. Near the house runs a small stream which enlivens the place. Here is a colliery belonging to the same person, which carrys on a good trade with the neighbouring country. New Dily <Dailly> is a small village, the lands about it rich and let as follows. Arable and meadow together from £0 6s 0d to £0 10 0d; the reason is they are old rents capable of great improvement and therefore the land sells at 40 years' purchase. Manure, marl, dung, earth and lime mixed. Oats sell at £0 18s 0d, barley £1 1s 0d, beans and peas £0 12s 0d per boll.

Ayr lyes 18 miles further, the country rich and fertile about it and lets: arable and meadow together from £0 5s 0d to £1 10s 0d per acre; sells at 30 years' purchase. Manure, lime, dung and earth mixed and seaweed. Barley sells at £0 15s 0d, oats £0 14s 0d to £0 15s 0d, beans and peas £0 16s 0d per boll. Labor, men 8d, women 4d and 5d the year round. Air is tolerably built, has a handsome bridge of 4 arches over the River Irwin, which divides Air from Cunningham. It was formerly a place of great trade, but now decayed. There is a good port, at the entrance of which is a large bay on each side and small key

<quay> for landing goods, close to which are the remains of a fortification erected by Cromwell, which commanded the entrance to the river, in which W[est] I[ndian] ships of no great burthen may ride safely. To this port belong 9 sail of Virginia and 19 other vessels, which carry coal to Dublin, herrings to Jamaica, merchandize to England, and bring back corn, provisions and merchandize from England. From the key you have a fine prospect of the highlands of the Isle of Arran and the flat coast of Lady Isle. Here is a manufactory of cheque handcherchiefs, lawns and stockings (but it being a fast day, the next being sacrament day, I could not see them), a neat tollbooth, a kirk encumbered with seats and an old house converted into an English church.

At this place, the mayor, seeing me writing in the street and making observations, prematurely concluded I was a spy and in consequence of his foolish conjecture applyed to the lieutenant of a troop of Lord G[eorge] Sackville's regiment quartered there to examine into the affair. Who, in obedience to the commands of the worthy magistrate, was about to execute the orders when the major of the regiment, Mr East, accidentally arrived in town, and the superiority being in him I was summoned downstairs just as I was going to bed by a very civil message from that gentleman desiring to speak to me. I was surprized at the unseasonableness of the request, and at great loss to conjecture the business a person could have to transact with me, who was an entire stranger to me in appearance. The first question asked me was my name, which being answered he told me he was sufficiently satisfied of the mayor's mistake and hoped I would excuse the affront and consider it as proceeding from an honest intention in the magistrate to perform his duty. The mystery being cleared up, after mutual civilities I retired to rest, the major and his brother officers to their bottle. I observed more people of the poorer sort with shoes and stockings at Air than in any other part of Scotland I had yet seen.

From Air to Irvine is 12 miles over the sands when the water is low. Here is a good harbor, to which between 70 and 80 sail belong. They trade to Ireland with coal (which the neighbouring hills abound with) and get money in return. To the W[est] I[ndies] they carry bale goods and bring back rum, sugar and mahogony. Over the River Irvine is a bridge of 4 arches. There is a good toolbooth. The country is flat, but rich; arable lets from £1 0s 0d to £2 0s 0d per acre, sells from 30 to 32 years' purchase. Manure is dung, lime and seaweed. Labor, 8d the whole year when constantly employed, when accidentally, from 10d to 1s. There are 2 rope walks and a sail cloth and handcherchief manufactory. A mile northeast of Irvine stands Eglington Castle, a poor aedifice, but the spatious plantations of furs that surround it are remarkably beautyfull. A mile further is the village of Kilwinnen, noted for the large ruins of an abbey. The country about it is very fruitfull and in general there are large crops of all sorts of grain, particularly oats.

Largis is 18 miles distant. We coasted it the chief part of the way and saw little worthy notice. 2 miles from it is a paultry house belonging to Lord Glasgow < Kelburn Castle >, placed on the side of a hill (close to the sea), one part of which is planted with furs, the rest covered with bushes. The village is as paultry as the house and so much out of repair that it would tempt one to beleive [it] the property of the same person. From hence there is a good view of the isles of Cumry and Bute, the first so clearly that any beast grazing there may be easily distinguished. Here the hay was standing in the field.

August 10th. Greenock is 15 miles. On my way thither fell a violent storm of rain, to avoid which I put my horse into a cottager's stable, who in coming out struck the saddle against the doorpost, which was so weakly fixed that it fell down and part of the wall with it. By this misfortune I was in danger of losing my horse and in all probability should have been obliged to have walked to my quarters had not 2 honest highlanders ventured to bring him out at the risque of their lives. As we proceeded on our journey we were most agreably entertained with several natural cascades, which the violence of the rain drove from the tops of the rocks. We had a fine view of Cathcart Isle and a pretty modern house belonging to Sir Michael Stewart <?Ardgowan House>, seated on an eminence at the entrance of a fertile vale which reaches to Greenock, filled with barley, oats and potatoes. A rivulet runs in the bottom and the hill is skirted with wood.

Greenock is built on the banks of the Clyd. At this place and Newport <Port Glasgow> are the ships belonging to the merchants of Glasgow unloaded and the goods carryed thither in hoys. Above the town are noble plantations of fir belonging to Sir Michael Stewart's son. 250 sail belong to this port and Newport, 30 of these of 500 tons burthen each, the property of the inhabitants of Greenock, which trade to the W[est] I[ndies] and America, exporting bale goods and the commodities of the country. In return bring rum, tobacco and sugar. From Lisbon they import wine and fruit. From Denmark, Sweden and Holland, timber and send them p[ar]t money, the rest in tobacco. From Virginia, logwood, tobacco and mahogony. From Jamaica, cotton. Here is a manufactory for making ropes, duck for sails, anchors and all things belonging to shipping. The herring fishery is carryed on here. There are 3 keys <quays>, east, west and middle, so placed that in the greatest storms ships in the harbour will ride safe. The east and west keys form a sort of crescent, between which the middle one shoots in a strait line, at which the ships are unloaded with great ease. Mr Steuart's house <?Greenock Mansion House> commands a good view of the town, harbour and opposite shore. Arable and meadow land together lets from £1 1s 0d to £1 10s 0d per acre, sells from 18 to 40 years' purchase. Labor £0 0s 8d per day in winter, £0 1s 0d in summer. Manure, street dirt, dung, lime and seaweed.

Port Glasgow is a small, neat town, better built than Greenock, but not so large, nor does it carry on so great trade. It is 3 miles distant and to Paisley 15 miles. The country is in some parts very stony and barren, in others pleasant and fruitfull and as we approached the town we saw several neat houses and plantations, particularly one belonging to Mr Campbell of <blank> <?Renfield>, executed with taste and judgement. There is a tunpike just begun to be made from Port Glasgow to Paisley. This is a populous town, extensive and well built, employs 1500 weavers in the linen trade. Here is the ruins of Paisley Abbey, formerly very rich. The body remains entire (and is converted into a church) and an upright of the window of the cross isle. The architecture is not of the rich Gothick. The whole belongs to Lord Dundonald, who has a ruinous old house and gardens adjoyning to it <The Place of Paisley>, tolerably situated with the River <blank> <Cart> at the bottom of them. The inhabitants are between 6000 and 7000. Here we saw a fair and horse race which had called together all the people of the country, which would have furnished a fine piece for the pencil of Hogarth or Teniers.

Glasgow is 6 miles distant, through the most beautyfull country in Scotland. A spirit of industry reigns in the neighbourhood and a de[sire] to set off everything to the best advantage. In every part you see gentlemen's houses neatly built, with large plantations to adorn their estates. Near the town grow wheat and turnips, the first we saw in Scotland. They sow them in rows with a small space between each row. This being left unsown serves instead of a summer fallow, so that every year the same quantity of ground is cultivated without it being necessary for the whole field to lye fallow.

Glasgow is situated in a fruitfull vale watered by the Clyd, which runs at the end of the town and over which is a bridge of 6 arches, the largest arch 70 feet high. The river is shallow, only navigable for hoys and small vessels, which bring up the goods from the ships at Greenock and Newport <Port Glasgow>. But there is a scheme in agitation for widening the river and raising the water by locks. On the side of the river is a handsome key for unloading goods. It is a place of great trade, being from their situation in some measure masters of the western branch. The number of manufactorys is as follows. Inkle or tape 2, for shoes [10; these] employs 500 men. Delft, glass; bottle and window, ditto. Damask linnens, muslin, lawn and gauze, iron ware. The delft made here will endure hot water without being boyled. In this the partys concerned have £8000 and the tape m[anufactory] sometimes costs £2000 per annum, besides the produce. ¾ of this belongs to Messrs Ingram and Lachford.

2 miles from Glasgow a manufactory for painting linen and cotton, to which the Company have lately annexed 100 looms. There is a tannery which employs a capital of £40,000, a large ropewalk secured by Act of Parliament, a mill for slitting iron bars. 2 miles from Glasgow a windmill for bruising bark the easier to tan leather, a public granary (belonging to the Bakers' Company) for keeping corn. The following hospitals: town's workhouse for 300 children and superannuated people; an infirmary (here all foreigners and other poor people accidentally in distress are relieved), below which is a mad house, arched over, indeed, to prevent the sick being disturbed, but notwithstanding must appear to be very improperly situated; Hutchinson's <Hospital> for old men, women and children; the Merchant's ditto for decayed merchants or their familyes (of this the steeple is fine); 2 ditto near the high church. The several markets are erected on pillars and so contrived that a pipe being placed in every 2nd pillar one pump will clean the whole place. To prevent filth, no butcher is allowed to kill in the town, but at the public slaughter house erected on the banks of the river. In a field close to the Clyd a wash house is erected at the public expence, where in winter the inhabitants are furnished with utensils and firing on paying a small fee of a halfpenny per tub.

In the town are 7 Scotch and 2 English established churches, 1 in the suburbs and 3 presbyterian meeting houses not established. St Andrew's is new built in the Composite Order and cost a great sum of money, but the stone is extremely bad, being in many places entirely green. The steeple is out of all proportion, being one third higher than it should be, but this is owing to the obstinacy and ignorance of the people, not to any blunder of the architect. In the middle of it the clock is placed and above and below it a large window to hide the deformity. The inside is neatly fitted up, the pulpit and reading desk being mahogony richly carved. The gallerys are faced with the same sort of wood, but the whole place is so filled with pews that the middle isle is quite blocked up and to prevent the capitals of the pillars, together with the architrave, freeze and cornice, from appearing discolored they have painted them, which has entirely spoiled the beauty of the church.

The entrance to St Mungo's is truly noble. As you come into the churchyard a large hill covered with tall furs suddenly presents itself to your view and gives great room to expect something grand, but no sooner do you step into the churchyard than you find yourself in danger of breaking your neck by the prodigious number of gravestones. The church itself is a stately aedifice of large extent and excellent workmanship, but seems never to have been entirely finished, for at the entrance into most cathedrals there are 2 towers, here only 1 appears compleat; another has been begun but small progress was made in it. The spire, in the rising out of a tower in the middle of a ragged cross, is much admired for its height and architecture. This building, the most perfect and noble remains of a cathedral in Scotland, is miserably spoiled, I might say defaced, within by the stupid contrivance of the people of Glasgow, who have divided it into 2 churches and filled them both with pews in such a manner that you have as little ability of stirring within as without. They have likewise very ingeniously walled up the grand entrance and obscured the windows by erecting monuments and railing them in. There are 2 chapter houses, one above the other; the west end, chapter house and dome are supported by a vault.

Near this stand the ruins of the archbishop's castle, now belonging to Major Cochran, who has pulled the building to pieces in order to sell the stone. There are 2 dye houses for blue only, which make to the amount of several thousand pounds per annum.

Whilst I am relating the particular beauties of this place I must pay due honor to the university or college founded by James the 2nd of Scotland 1453. It consists of 2 old c[our]ts and 1 new c[our]t, where the professors live, a handsome library elegantly finished, the inside well filled with printed books and manuscripts. The length is about 54, the breadth 20 feet. There is a gallery round the upper part of the room supported by pillasters, and 2 fluted pillars at each end of the Ionic Order. In the passage below the 2nd c[our]t and garden are cases filled with Roman inscriptions taken out of the Roman Wall. There is a large garden belonging and adjoining to the college and at some little distance an observatory now erecting, at each end a gallery ornamented with a ballustrade (from whence there is a good view of the town) and in the middle of the gallery an opening is left for fixing the instruments of observation.

The scholars educated here chiefly lodge in the town, though they may have rooms in college paying from 8s to 2 guineas per annum for them according to their goodness. There are no commons, but the professors and the porter keep tables at which they may dine, or at their own rooms. Every professor gives a course of lectures in his own science, to which he is confined by the original charter, though formerly every professor instructed his scholars in different sciences. Each scholar pays for a course of lectures £1 11s 6d, the law excepted, which is £3 3s 0d; many give more according to their fortunes. They begin October 10th and end June 10th. The scholars are divided into different classes and ascend gradually. They pay for only 2 courses, the rest are given gratis. There is an estate left for the benefit of Scotsmen educated here and sent afterwards to Baliol College, Oxford, after residing here 2 years at least. They have £40 per annum for 11 years; the presentation is in Glasgow College. The estate is worth £900 per annum.

All the professors and several other persons have formed a literary society at which they meet once a week from November to May in the evening, where they alternately produce an English dissertation, on which when read the rest of the company offer their remarks; sometimes they offer questions instead of the dissertation. This lasts 3 hours. In the first c[our]t of the college there is a school for painting, for which purpose the managers have purchased a large collection of pictures abroad and copied some of the most eminent masters' celebrated pieces in order that the scholars may be the better instructed; another room for engraving, 3rd, 4th and 5th for moulding in plaister and modelling and copying. For these noble attempts to erect seminarys of arts of these sorts the public are indebted to the abilities, labor and industry of those 2nd race of the Stephens's,[6] Messrs Robert and Andrew Foulis, who with the assistance of 3 merchants were enabled to make this collection of pictures, to whom they pay an annual stipend for their shares and take the whole management upon themselves. They have now 20 scholars, who contribute nothing but are paid for their labor. There is likewise a rolling press for casting off prints.

I wish it was in my power to congratulate either of our English universities upon having amongst them such public spirited men, who will always be held in veneration for their attention to literature and desire of cultivating polite arts. Nor will gratitude permit me to pass over in silence the civilities I received from them, and doubt not that all strangers will meet with the same obligeing behavior from them and the professors, particularly Messrs Moor and Smyth,[7] the first professor of Greek, the last of Humanity.

The town is extremely well built with great regularity and the new houses with magnificence. They are fond of piazzas, which are usefull and ornamental, but liable to make the lower part of the houses dark. The chief public aedifices worthy notice are the exchange, tolbooth and guardroom with a colonnade, which is at first appearance pretty, but liable to many objections when viewed by the rules of proportion. The inhabitants at a moderate computation of 5 persons in each family are estimated at 40,000. It is remarkable that in the first 8 months of the present war the merchants of this town lost upwards of £120,000, notwithstanding which no one has yet failed, though the losses have been since very great.

From Glasgow I went over to see Hamilton House, 8 miles distant, which is a magnificent palace, more suitable to a crowned head than a subject. It was built in Charles 2nd's reign and was intended to be a compleat H, thereby indicating the owner, <but> the original plan is as yet but half carried into execution and resembles a U. The inside is highly finished and consists of several handsome apartments in the wings. The front is entirely taken up with the gallery, 118 feet by 22 feet, in which are several good portraits and other pictures.

Amongst them the following are the most remarkable: 1 *A Treaty of Peace between Spain and England after the Armada*; the portraits represented are 3 Spaniards, 5 English and 3 Dutchmen sitting at a table, all fine portraits, great expression and good drawing, unusually dark. 2 *Duke of Hamilton Beheaded*, Vandyke, well drawn. 3 *Dukes of Hamilton and Lauderdale in One Picture* prodigiously fine, by C Johnson <Cornelis Janssens>; the Duke of Lauderdale gives a scroll of paper to Duke Hamilton. 4 *Daniel in the Lyons' Den*, Rubens, large and very fine, extremely natural, great expression of the lions, some tame; one makes full at him and then stops. 5 *Gustavus Adolphus*, Vandyke, very fine. 6 *Lord Basil Hamilton*, governor of Jamaica, first Earl of Denbigh in an Indian dress, shooting, Vandyke, very fine. 7, 8, 9 three large Titian's, exceedingly fine, viz. *Disciples at Emaus*, *Taking Down from the Cross* and *Burying Christ*. 10 a *Holy Family*, uncertain whom, 2 boys, Christ and John, round and inexpressibly beautyfull. 11 *Madonna*, in a contemplative posture, Guido, color and expression very sweet. 12 *Holy*

Family, uncertain: espousal of St Katherine, Virgin Mary with Christ in her arms, St Peter with his keys and St John represented 50 years old. 13 *Vandyke* by himself, question, too dark, wants brilliancy, not in his manner? 14 *Christ Crowned with Thorns*, uncertain, good.

The town of Hamilton is tolerably neat. There is a new church built by the late Duke Hamilton, instead of one which he pulled down because it stood close to his house. The buryal place of the family still remains, with one monument, but is in sad repair. The park is said to be 10 miles round, but as it stood at some distance from the house I did not go thither. In it are said to be some wild cows, milk white, the only beasts of the kind in Great Britain. Upon a hill in the park before the house the last Duke's father built a dog kennel in representation of triumphal arches; it is called Chateleraud. In the churchyard is kept a black American bear and a lyon in a building adjoyning. The ground immediately adjacent to the house is quite neglected. The approach to the town from Glasgow is truly majestic, through an avenue of pines a mile in length; at the end of it a bridge over the Clyd, where there is a toll gate so handsome that a traveller would naturally suppose that it was the entrance to a royal park and must be surprized at the demand of a penny for leave to pass. The whole way to Glasgow is fruitfull and pleasant, agreably diversifyed with plantations of furs and to which you ride 5 or 6 miles on the banks of the Clyd.

The next trip I made was to Kilsyth, 15 miles from Glasgow, a mean dirty village in a disagreable country surrounded with barren hills, which carry you quite to Sterling, 15 miles more; another indifferent town which formerly engrossed the trade of the highlands, but is much decayed since the military roads were made across the highlands, whose inhabitants now furnish themselves at Glasgow. Here I saw the ruins of Lord Mar's palace, lately sold by Mr Erskine to be pulled down. The castle is entire, though supposed to be much stronger than in fact it is, because the rebels beseiged it without effect. The military say it would soon be reduced if a train of artillery was brought against it, notwithstanding they may command the country from the castle. The reason is that there is no cover for the men to serve the guns, on which account a few shells thrown from the other side of the hill southeast of the castle would soon drive them away, or a few shot would beat the masonry about their ears. Besides, the fortification is not kept in good repair. Here are the buildings where formerly the Scots parliaments were held, the king's palace and chapel, all now converted either to barracks or storehouses. From the castle wall on a clear day may be seen distinctly Edinburgh Castle. The windings of the Forth are so many and intricate that a stranger would imagine that there were 2 or 3 rivers. Here is a manufactory of plaid, stockings and linnen.

We passed the Forth at Stirling Bridge and entered immediately upon the king's road which leads into the highlands. In our way to Crief we passed by Castle Drummond, formerly the seat of Lord Perth, but forfeited to the Crown by his attainder. It is built on a high hill at some distance from the road, surrounded on every side with extensive plantations of furs and other trees, which appear to great advantage in that barren, mountainous country. Crief is a poor village 19½ miles distant from Stirling.

About 5 miles on the other side we entered the Vale of Glen Almond, where the mountains on each side are remarkably steep and high, though the height is not near so great as Rutherford, in his plan of the military roads,[8] asserts when, in order to surprize his reader, he has the modesty to say the pass between these mountains is so narrow and the hills so high that the sun is seen but 2 or 3 hours in the longest day. I will not affirm this to be false, but I own I have great reason to beleive it is not true, for when I passed it, August 15th (which is almost 2 months after the sun has been at its greatest height), at 27 minutes past 3 the sun was apparent during our passage, except at one particular point of the highest mountain. From this you ascend several miles through a miserable country where nothing presents itself but black, barren hills riseing above each other, after which you have as disagreable a descent for 3 miles. At the end of it you fall into the beautyfull Vale of Strathtay, and having passed the noble bridge < at Aberfeldy > built by Marshal Wade over the river of the same name you come to Weem, the seat of Sir Robert Menzies, at the bottom of a very high mountain covered with wood from top to bottom. The natural beauties about it are fine, but it owes little to judgement or taste. At 2 miles distance we forded the Water of Lyon.

To Kenmore, 25 miles from Crief. The land in this neighbourhood is of a light soil. Arable lets at £0 10s 0d per acre. Land sells at 25 years' purchase. Labor in summer is from 2½d to 3d per day and victuals, or 6d without. In winter they are glad to work for their victuals only and what the person is willing to give. Barley is £0 12s 0; oats £0 9s 0d, potatoe seed £0 10s 8d per boll.

Adjoyning to this village is Lord Broadalbain's < Breadalbane's > seat called Taymouth, in the midst of a large grove near the river of the same name and surrounded with prodigious mountains of stone, which the present lord has endeavoured to cover by sowing and planting fur and furze. In some places he has succeeded, though they thrive slowly on that side which is most exposed to the sun; the other flourishes extremely, being in some parts an entire wood disposed into walks, and buildings are placed very judiciously to take different views. The entrance from the village is upon the south terrace an English mile in length, 45 feet wide; along the banks of the Tay and on the north side another terrace is making 50 feet wide, which when carryed to the point of Lyon will be 3 miles long. It consists of different plants, as fur, oak, birch, mountain ash, broom, beech, laurel, spirea [frutex] < *Spiraea salicifolia* >, larix and many others. There is a beech tree in these enclosures 5 feet diameter, 15 feet in circumference, and several large sycamores.

There is a paddock for tame deer and another in which are 3 roebucks and 1 doe so wild that on hearing the least noise they run away and will not suffer themselves to be seen if they can avoid. They are rather larger than common deer and resemble them in their colour. They are taken with great difficulty in the mountains near Kenmore, which abound with them.

The house is situated in a bottom, with a handsome lawn in front. Beyond that appear the mountains on the south in a semicircle lined with wood. The body of the house is very old, the 2 wings new, joined to the body by a close colonnade; they were added by the late lord. The inside is neatly fitted up and has a great number of rooms; a saloon 40 feet by 22 with a recess of fluted Doric pillars, a drawing room hung with tapestry presented Lord Broadalbain by the King of Denmark, the colours well preserved, and a library of good books. There is an extensive kitchen garden walled round and filled with good fruit. The peaches, plumbs and cherries very small, apricots as large as in England. From the south terrace you have a view of the village 3 miles up the loch and the isle in it.

Loch Tay is 15 miles long and belongs to Lord Broadalbain, whose house is at one end and who has an old castle < Finlarig Castle > at the other, where he retired when the rebels in 1745 came in pursuit of him. In this loch near Kenmore there is an isle < Isle of Loch Tay > planted with wood, where are the ruins of the monastry of Kinnegary.[9] Lord Broadalbain's estate reaches 70 miles quite into Argyleshire.

The labourers' annual pay here is £2 0s 0d in money and 6½ bolls of meal, which at the lowest price is £0 10s 0d per boll = £3 5s 0d; at the highest £1 0s 0d = £6 10s 0d. 2 miles from Kenmore we passed by a beautyfull natural cascade called Kaltrey Waterfall. The water comes first from a hill into a bason, thence amongst a heap of large stones with great violence and lastly into the bed of the river.

To Delnachairdich < Dalnacardoch > is 20 miles (through a disagreable mountainous country), where the Dunkell and

Stirling roads join, and thence to Blair 10 miles more. Here is the seat of the Duke of Athol, situated near a vale through which flows a branch of the River Garry. This castle, 550 years old, was made a garrison for the king's forces in 1745 by Sir Andrew Agnew, whom a part of the rebel army blockaded there several days in hopes of taking it, but without success. To avoid this for the future the Duke has now dismantled the castle so as to render it untenable and converted it to a habitable house only, which he is fitting up and furnishing in the most elegant manner. He has likewise added 2 straight wings which contains several handsome bedchambers etc.

In the old castle are a dineing room 36 feet long 27 feet broad and 18 feet high, and on the 2nd storey a magnificent ballroom 52 feet long, breadth 30 feet, height 23 feet, furnished with crimson damask and most richly carved; the cieling coved and elegantly stuccoed. The windows do not give sufficient light, the walls being 9 feet thick. There are few except family pictures, amongst which the most remarkable are *The Prince of Orange and the Earl of Tullybardin*, date 1606. There are likewise on the staircase two whole lengths of *Robert Bruce 1st*, the 97th king of Scotland, dated 1306, and *Fergus, the First King of Scotland*, who reigned 335 years before Christ. There is a bed said to be worked by the Dutchess de la Tremouille, daughter to the Prince of Orange and Lady Derby, her daughter, set on white cloth, the bed posts Gothic pillars. There is a gallery which communicates with every room.

Before the house is a small stream resembling a gutter in summer, over which are built no less than 3 common and Chinese bridges, all within the space of 300 yards; the reason of this I am at a loss to conjecture. The kitchen garden is the best disponed I ever saw; it is situated on a declivity on both sides, between which is a canal the whole length of it, with several small islands. At the end is a prospect house commanding a fine view of the whole, together with the castle; the whole is 9 acres. There is a wilderness filled with all sorts of forest trees and evergreens, 60 acres in extent. The kitchen garden is forced ground made on a rock and is computed to cost £70 per acre. On the other side is a summer house fitted up with larix wood, the growth of this place. The vale below is rich ground; through it flows the River Banvil.

From Blair to Dunkell is 20 miles, the best and pleasantest ride in this part of Scotland, being chiefly through woods of birch on the side of a mountain, at the bottom whereof flows the Garry to Killicranky Pass, where it loses itself in the Timmel and a little lower both fall into the Tay. On the opposite side are hills finely wooded and meadows in the bottom. Killicranky is famous for the defeat of Lord Dundee in King William's reign. It is admirably situated for a small army to defend against a more numerous body of men, being extremely narrow and environed with stupendous mountains on each side. In one part is a handsome waterfall, but as the season was dry we did not see it to advantage.

At Dunkell the military road enters the mountains. Here the Duke of Athol has another neat house < Dunkeld House >, which appears like a villa belonging to his palace of Blair. He is building large offices here, into every part of which water is conveyed in leaden pipes. At the distance of almost an English mile, adjoining to, or rather enclosed in, the garden, are the ruins of the cathedral, formerly dedicated to St Columba, almost entire on the outside. The Duke is making great plantations, or rather forming a new country, here; likewise on each side of the road, over which he has thrown a bridge of communication. Land sells at 30 years' purchase. Labor 6d per day. Dunkell a market town; the houses are very good, being mostly new built and slated, not like their neighbours miserable huts covered with heath, earth and turf. On the other side of the Tay, almost close to the town, is the hill where once flourished Burnham Wood (mentioned by Shakespear in his *Tragedy of Macbeth*) (10 miles distant from Duncy Nane < Dunsinane >), now a barren mountain.

To Perth is 15 miles. The road thither is for the most part good and pleasant, the country being well cultivated. In our way we passed through a noble plantation and had a distant view of the house <House of Nairne>, lately the estate of Lord Nairn, but now forfeited to the government by the share he had in the late rebellion.

We crossed the Tay near Perth to vizit the palace of Scone (where the Old Pretender in 1715 acted a royal farce for a small space of time), where formerly the Scotch kings kept their c[our]t. The front is long and regular with the ends projecting a little; it consists only of one story containing a gallery 170 feet long, 18 broad, the cieling circular, with the remains of it having once been painted. The King's and Queen Mary's beds still remain, though in a great danger of an expulsion from the moths, unless like their monarch they abdicate or are removed. In the same bedchamber (James 7th <?6th>) is some beautyfull tapestry, well preserved, said to be the work of Queen Mary; the cielings are all stuccoed and the chimneypieces very fine. These are the only remains of royal grandeur, the other apartments being entirely gutted, unless a few signpost portraits can with justice merit the appellation of furniture. This palace, with the grounds round it, are the property of Lord Stormount, one of whose ancestors has a noble monument in the church, which is almost as ruinous as the palace. The situation of the palace is very pleasant on the banks of the Tay. It is built round 2 courts, but the rooms are too small and mean. The town through which you go to it consists of a few poor huts covered with turf, whose inhabitants seem to be courtiers, well adapted to the neighbouring aedifice.

Perth is a large town consisting of several good streets. Though not well built, it has a market, a linnen manufactory and partakes of the weaving trade. Land lets there for £2 0s 0d to £2 10s 0d per acre.

15 miles further lyes Kinross, the road to it through a fertile country, the produce beans, peas, oats, barley and potatoes,

generally fine crops of each. Kinross is a burgh town, the interest in Sir John Bruce, who has a handsome seat <Kinross House> close to it built in a good taste. There is a good hall, dining room and staircase; I would add ballroom upstairs, but a very small proportion of that part of the house is finished, being only bare. The garden produces hay and barley instead of fruit and flowers. The approach is through 2 large groves, but this greatly hurt by 2 pavilions which perform the office of stables. The back of the house is planted with furr and other trees, but the winds have demolished some of them entirely and makes continual attacks on the rest.

Close to these is Loch Leven, said to be 11 computed miles round. In it is an island with an old castle where Queen Mary was once confined by her rebellious subjects. This lake, with the land that borders on it on every side, belongs to Sir John Bruce. The land that lyes near the lake and is in Sir John's occupation is sadly neglected and overrun with the weeds. Round the town of Kinross arable and meadow consolidated let at £1 16s 8d per acre. Land sells at 30 years' purchase. Labor 6d and 7d per day.

To Queensferry on the Tay <Forth> is 15 miles through a country equally pleasant and fertile. About a mile from it we passed through the royal burgh of Innerkethan <Inverkeithing>, a mean, miserable, paultry town, teaching us what we were to expect from its neighbouring villages, especially the fishing town of North Queensferry; 10 sail belongs to it. Land lets for £0 12s 0d to £0 14s 6d per acre, sells for 24 to 30 years' purchase. Labor from 6d to 8d or 4d and victuals. An isle in the Tay <Forth> and old castle <?Rosyth Castle> ruined by Cromwell. Here we passed over the Tay <Forth>, 2 miles broad, to South Queensferry.

To Hopton <Hopetoun> is 3 miles. The house is a most stately edifice having 21 windows in front, on each side open colonnades with ballustrade and vases at top to connect the wings, of 7 windows each, to the body of the house. They were built many years since the body by Adams < William Adam >. The north wing consists of stables, the south a library 94 feet long, 37 broad, 29 high, being the whole depth of the wing. Besides this 2 other small rooms, at top of each a cupola. The inside is fitting up with equal grandeur. The first room is a hall 33 feet long, 22 broad. In it are 4 statues, 2 of them *Minerva* and *Venus*, and 15 busts, 4 of them very small and placed over the 2 doors, in general well preserved. The dining room 33 feet by 30, the cieling coved and ornamented with festoons and an architrave, freeze and cornice. 2 good *Battle Pieces*, small, but well painted; a *Boy at Full Length with a Dog*, strong expression and very fine. A drawing room 42 feet by 21, cieling coved and richly ornamented in stucco; architrave etc to be gilt. The pictures are: *St Francis*, girt with a cord, praying to the Virgin Mary, who appears in the clouds with Our Saviour in her arms, the expression in his countenance extremely fine; such agony mixt with such devotion, the whole appearance so melancholly, with death's head and a rock; the colouring is equal to the expression. 2 small pieces of *Ruins*, pretty. 4 *Musicians with Instruments*, well executed. *The Resurrection of Our Saviour*, a large and capital piece, surprize of the soldiers inimitable, exprest a thousand ways. A *Portrait* in the manner of Titian. A bedchamber 25½ by 18 feet. Here the *Portrait of an Old Woman* in Rembrandt's best manner, at bottom marked S K 1639; she holds a missal in her hand, which she has been reading. Another fine *Portrait* although not equal to the former.

Beyond the great dining room a bedchamber and antichamber, from which you pass through the hall to a winding staircase in an octagon with a cupola by way of skylight, and thence to the common eating parlour 27 by 24 feet, fitted up in a plain manner. Over the doors are 8 small marble busts and on the chimney several bronzes. Above these *The Representation of St Romoald*, very fine, not large, coloring and drawing bears a strong resemblance to Andrea Sacchi's manner; expression good. 2 Rosa of Tivoli and several heads well executed. In a closet adjoyning 2 antique busts over the chimney. On the other side of the eating parlour a drawing room hung with tapestry, finely executed and well preserved; wainscot and doors richly carved and gilt. Cieling coved but plain. The south wing consists of 4 small rooms and a passage. The back front to the garden is not regular, having more windows on one side than the other and a projection on each side of the door, which is disagreable to the eye.

The extent of the garden or (as, the Scotch call, enclosures) polishes <policies> is 40 acres, miserably laid out, without the least taste. The whole spot is on an eminence close to the Tay <Forth>, planted with formal woods through which a narrow cut permits you now and then with difficulty to view the river. Precise clipt hedges and evergreen birds bear a great share in this ill concerted plan. In one part of the plantation is a small raised plot of ground where once stood the castle of Abercorn, from whence a noble peer of the name of Hamilton derives his title. Adjacent to the garden is the deer park, a spot without one single grove to shelter the herd, and ½ a mile further stands Blackness Castle, garrisoned by a sergeant and 15 men; the governor, Lord Hopton's brother. The extent of the plantations, exclusive of the garden, is 60 acres. The ground in front of the house is too narrow to be compleatly elegant, being straightened by the river on the north. The price land lets for in this part is heath £0 5s 0d, arable £2 0s 0d, meadow, £1 0s 0d; sells at 30 years' purchase. Labor 7d per day.

To Edinburgh is 13½ miles through a fertile country producing oats, barley, wheat and potatoes in great quantities, with many gentlemen's seats dispersed up and down. To Dalkeith and back to Edinburgh is 12 miles through a very pleasant and fertile part of the county. Dalkeith is a dirty, ill-built town remarkable only for the Duke of Buccleugh's seat <Dalkeith House> and park, which is close to one end of it, seated on a hill, with a deep vale behind it, through which runs a tolerable stream and the other side covered with noble woods. A little expense would make it a very magnificent place, but the present fashion among the nobles of this country of residing chiefly in England is an insuperable objection to bestowing any part of their receipts in improving their estates here. We were told that we could not see the house (it being Sunday), but might walk in the park.

A mile further is another tolerable house belonging to the same noble duke, through which you pass from one park to the other by an avenue of larix trees near a mile in extent. This place is called East Park. It consists of several good rooms and has a gallery remarkably long and narrow filled with portraits well painted, viz. *Duchess of Mazarine, ditto her Mother, Nell Gwyn, Lady Eglington, Duchess of Bedford, Lady Carlisle* etc, the story of *Tomyris cutting off Cyrus's Head* and *Sea Nymphs bringing Offerings to a Young Man.*

Between Dalkeith and Edingburgh is a good house < The Drum > and plantations belonging to Lord Somerville, who has disposed them in a judicious manner. The house is small, but neatly fitted up in the Chinese taste; it commands a fine view of the Forth and North Berwick Law. Here are 2 good pictures of the *Seaton Family* and the *Princess of Orange.* Near the house is set up the cross of Edinburgh, which was lately taken down there to make room for some ignoble buildings. In a tour I made to Elphinstone I called at New Hales, the seat of Sir David Dalrymple, where I found a small and convenient habitation furnished with great elegance; there is a noble library filled with books in every science.

The places at Edinburgh worthy notice are the castle, a regular fortification seated upon a high rock commanding the city and adjacent country, and has hitherto been esteemed impregnable against canon, though I beleive without reason; at least it is not in that high reputation amongst the military. It is kept in good repair, has an armoury and several spare field pieces mounted ready for service. The building where the parliament was formerly held is now appropriated to different uses.

One division is fitted with shops (like those in Westminster Hall), behind which is the bailey's court; the other half is the court of the Lord Ordinary, who tries causes of small value in the first instance, where one of the ordinary judges sits every week in session time. In an adjoining room are the 14 judges or Lords of Session, the supreme civil judicature in Scotland. In the lower part of the Parliament House is a library of books and manuscripts belonging to the advocates. In the square before this aedifice is a good statue of Charles 2nd on horseback. Not far from this the city are building an Exchange, the ground of which it is said cost £12,000 and the whole expence it is thought will amount to £32,000. It is built in a miserable taste and, like the Mansion House at London, will, I fear, be a monument to shew the incapacity of bodies corporate to act with propriety and taste. Near the castle is a public reservoir for the use of the city, which is brought 3 miles in lead pipes into a large copper cistern which contains 250 tons of water.

The palace of Holyroodhouse is a handsome building erected at different times; it is esteemed the most compleat in the kingdom. It is divided into separate lodgings, where several of the nobility have their apartments, except the chief rooms of state, which are not used by any person and remain entirely unfurnished. Amongst these the gallery is most remarkable, being 147 feet long, 28 broad, 18 high and adorned with the portraits of Scotch Kings. In Duke Hamilton's apartment we were shewed Queen Mary's Bedchamber, where Rizzio was murdered and afterwards thrown on the floor of a dark gallery or landing place, which was so stained with the blood that all methods have hitherto proved ineffectual to remove it. *Sic nugae aniles Scotiae*. In Lord Broadalbain's < Breadalbane's > apartments are the following Vandykes: *Cavendish, Duke of Newcastle*, whole length; *Villiers, Duke of Buckingham (small head and shoulders); Ditto and Family*, very fine; *Earls of Warwick and Holland*, whole lengths. Behind the palace is the conventual church, an ancient building. It has been for some time in ruins, but is now repairing for divine service. The persons employed are endeavouring to make it as dark and unsightly as possible by stopping up the upper windows with stone. The park is 4 miles round, has neither tree nor deer, is only fit for pasture. In it stands Arthur's Seat, near ½ a mile high. The palace and park is sanctuary for debtors.

Heriot's Hospital is a magnificent building and noble foundation for an indefinite number of freemen's sons, who are maintained, cloathed and educated untill they are fit for apprenticeships, or to go to the universities, where they are allowed handsome exhibitions. It owes its being to George Heriot, jeweller to James 6th, who left £17,000 in trust to Dr Balcanqual to dispose of in pious uses, which he did by building and endowing this house. The Royal Infirmary is another mark of the benevolence of all sorts of people, who contributed money and labor towards erecting this beautyfull aedifice for the reception of maimed and diseased poor. Therein are hot and cold baths, an amphitheatre for the students in surgery to attend in at amputations (built in the manner of that in Mugwell <Monkwell> Street, London, which Inigo Jones designed). The wards and other rooms are kept with the utmost cleanlyness and order.

There is a playhouse, concert room and assembly room, all admirably conducted, particularly the 2 last. At the concert each steward has a liberty of giving a ticket for admitting 1 stranger in winter, but in summer that liberty is extended according to the number of subscribers who are in town. At the assembly a lady presides, to whose order every one pays implicit obedience. As the company is generally numerous, it is a rule to divide them into sets and each set may dance only one or two dances as the lady patroness ordains, who gives each couple a ticket appointing the set and couple they belong to, and by this method prevents many quarrels about precedency, that terrible disturber of society.

The houses of the nobility are paultry and mean, the inns

indifferent, generally adapted only for the service of beasts, men being obliged to lodge at private houses, the New Inn excepted, which accomodates both extremely well. The streets are narrow, the houses ill built and immoderately high, some amounting to 14 stories, though they chiefly consist of 6. This is occasioned by the extravagent price at which ground sells. Hence arises that abominable custom of throwing out of the windows every night the ordure of the family to avoid going down stairs, so that passengers who are abroad at these hours must act with great circumspection for fear of suffering from the vollies of chamber pots and close stools from above, or wading through excrement below. Another insufferable inconvenience is the croud of beggars that fill the streets without the city gates and assault passengers with their impetuous demands of charity.

The university was founded 1580 by James 6th. It consists of 3 courts, built in a very mean and irregular manner. Its particular professorships and methods of government I am unable to describe, having had no opportunity of informing myself of them. The collegiate church of St Giles is divided into several places of devotion. It is tolerably built, but the architects have contrived to make it appear heavy and disagreable to the eye by means of a tower formed in the shape of an imperial crown. It is remarkable for a set of bells which are not rung out as in England, but played upon by the hand with keys like a harpsichord, the person playing having great leather covers to his fists by which he can strike with greater force. They play all manner of tunes; the present tune in vogue is *God Save Great George* etc. The town gives the man a yearly salary for playing upon them from 12 to 1 every day, Sundays and Holy Days excepted.

Having now noted the several places at Edinburgh which appeared to me most worthy observation, I cannot leave it without expressing a due sense of the civilities I received, particularly from Lord Haddington, [?Major] Stevenson, George Innes and Stewart and many others, but from none with greater hospitality and politeness than Lord Aberdower, who carried us to Dalmahoy, a seat of Lord Moreton's, where we spent 2 days in a most agreable manner.

The house is small and not yet entirely fitted up, but those rooms that are furnished are compleated very elegantly. The situation is good, being in a fine champion country. There are several good pictures, viz. *Lord Moreton*, the inventor of The Maiden, himself beheaded by that engine; half length of *Queen Mary*, an original painted when she was confined in Loch Leven; *Lord Pembroke*, whole length, Vandyke; a *Church with People Praying*, Holbein's manner; *Portrait in a Turk's Dress*, half length, Rembrandt, very good; a *bozzo* by ditto; *View of the Glassieres or Ice Mountains in Switzerland*, ditto, very singular and finely executed; a *Holy Family*, Solimeni; *Alpheus and Arethusa*, Andrea Saachi, an original and very capital; an *Ascension* by Teniers after P Veronese, very singular; *Cattle* etc, Castiglioni. The environs round the house are planted very judiciously, particularly the fields, which are flanked on every side by a walk 20 feet wide, a plantation 80 feet and another walk beyond that 20 feet; and these are so contrived as to preserve a communication through the whole farm without the trouble of opening a gate or passing through a field. From the house you have a fine view of Edinburgh Castle and Arthur's Seat.

From hence you pass through a fertile country to Glasgow, 45 miles distant from Edinburgh and 10 miles further to Dumbarton, one of the most pleasant rides in the world along the banks of the Clyd through a beautyfull country filled with the seats of merchants and noblemen. The castle is situated on a high rock on the edge of the Clyd, accessible only on the side towards the river and out of the reach of canon, but like that at Edinburgh would be reduced by throwing in shells; otherwise famine alone must force it to surrender. It seems now to be only of use against any insurrection and to keep the country quiet.

2 miles farther, on the River Leven, is a small village called Boniel < Bonhill >, from a hill just above which there is a pleasant view over the Clyd on one side; on the other Loch Lomond and the windings of the Leven. Having crossed the river we rode on the banks of this beautyfull loch to Luss 8 miles, a small, poor village remarkable for its being the entrance to the western highlands (where the military road commences) and its vicinity to Loch Lomond. Here we embarked to vizit the principal islands. The first was Inchnolaig, high land and filled with yew trees; it belongs to Sir James Colqhoun, who keeps there 100 head of wild deer of the red sort. Inchonnangan is a most delightfull spot plantd with firrs, which form a compleat wood. Inchdavanan < Inchtavannach > is planted with oaks, which is very profitable to the owner, who at every cutting gets 7000 marks. Not far from this is a small island with a ruin covered with ivy < ?Inchgalbraith >, on the top of which an eagle constantly builds her nest. These belong likewise to Sir James Colquhon. Inchmurin is the chief island in the lake, being 2½ miles long; it contains corn, pasture and wood and abounds with red deer. It is the property of the Duke of Montrose (who has a seat < Buchanan > on the opposite shore), as well as several other islands. This beautyfull lake is esteemed the largest of fresh water in Scotland, being 24 miles long, 8 miles broad and emptyes itself in the Clyd by the Leven.

Here we were witness of the truth of the report peculiar to this water, where are waves without wind. At the time we were upon it there was not a breath of air and yet the water rose in waves like the sea to our great surprize. It is said to contain 30 islands. On the opposite side stands a mountain of the same name (Ben Lomond) of a prodigious height, overshadowing all the neighbouring rocks. The way to it is very irksome and in some places so steep that we were obliged to crawl on hands and knees. From the beginning of the ascent to the summit is 5 English miles. In several parts we sunk up to our knees in mire. We were fortunate enough to have a fine day and from

Inveraray Castle, Argyll. Engraved view after drawing by Moses Griffith, c. 1769. *(Reproduced by permission of the RCAHMS)*

the top on one side could see Edinburgh and Sterling Castles at 40 miles distance. On the other that of Dumbarton, Port Glasgow, the Clyde and all the country beyond, many miles.

About 2 miles from our landing place we experienced the hospitality of the laird of Blairvochy who, though a poor farmer and laboring at his harvest, left his work to entertain us with the best fare his cot afforded. It consisted of sour milk and goats' whey which, homely as it was, we received with greater pleasure, and it was more acceptable to us, than all the dainties of a palace. The heartiness with which he welcomed us was so sincere that I should esteem myself guilty of the highest ingratitude if I did not pay him his due applause. Having furnished me with a little horse that carried me to the steep part of the hill (where I was obliged to dismount), an advantage my companions would not have been averse to, when I got within a 100 yards of the top I had the misfortune to be seized with a dizziness, which prevented my quixotism being carried to so great a height as that of my friends, who feasted very heartily on the summit, whilst I was descending with the utmost caution, or rather creeping down on all fours. Having returned safely with assistance to the first resting place and refreshed myself with the relicts of their repast we all set out together and by bogtrotting with rapidity arrived at our hospitable laird's without any other accident, except being much dirted. Here we found a fresh entertainment of chicken and potatoes provided for us, with a draught of the whey and buttermilk, which having finished we returned to our quarters at Luss. Land lets from 12s to 20s per acre. Manure, dung and lime.

The road to Tarbot is on the side of the same lake and affords every moment different views of the islands and that stupendous mountain above mentioned, which overtops its craggy neighbours. The road is cut through the side of a mountain, likewise encompassed on each side with wood. At Tarbot we turned off to the left (the right leading on the king's road to Fort William) and having left these enchanting scenes soon came in view of

Loch Long, a salt water lake which, coasting near two miles, we entered Glen Crow, remarkable only for the most savage and barbarous appearance, where the military found it so difficult to make the roads through the steepness of the hills, or rather craggs of stone, that they have formed on the top an amphitheatre of turf and fixed up a stone with this inscription: *Rest and be Thankfull.* Here you enter Glen Kinglas, equally horrible, barbarous and disagreable. At Cairndow you come to Loch Fine, another salt-water lake more extensive and pleasant than Loch Long.

From hence we had a very agreable ride of 10 miles to Inverary, a neat highland town seated close to the shore. This, together with some others, sends a member to parliament. Here we were indebted to the politeness of Mr Campbel of Ashnisch <Asknish> and Mr Richardson <John Richardson, the provost>, who presented us with the freedom of the burgh and shewed us everything that could afford us entertainment, of which the castle of Inverary was the chief subject. It is built in the manner of the old castles in the time of Henry 2nd and in some particulars is said to bear a strong resemblance to Solomon's Temple. The front is 150 by 138 feet; each corner swells into a large round. The whole is built in the Gothic manner with battlements at top. It stands in a sunk fosse, which goes round the house and among many other good effects has this, that no servants appear, except those who must necessarily attend, nor are any of the transactions or business of the family apparent above stairs. So much care is taken about these particulars that loaded carts pass through a subterraneous passage to the fosse, over which the entrance to the house from the northeast and southwest is by a bridge over 2 beautyfull Gothic arches with balustrades on each side at top, neatly ornamented and terminated at the end by 2 conical pillars. The stone of which this castle is built is a sort of slate stone which bears a good polish and catches the fog so strongly that it is supposed to be proof against weather. The slate is brought from Eisdall, upon the west coast opposite to Mull and belongs to Lord Broadalbain < Breadalbane >, and the stone from the opposite side of Loch Fine.

The rooms are well contrived and calculated to contain a numerous family. The principal are a gallery 110 feet long, 22½ feet broad, 20 feet high; dining room, 45 feet by 25 feet; drawing room 30 by 21; saloon 34 feet by 24 feet and 75 feet high. It is placed in the middle of the house and reaches to the top; on the 2nd floor are 2 open arches through which light is communicated on the sides from windows in the middle tower. On each side is a geometrical staircase, which preserves a communication with every single room on the 2nd floor by means of a gallery which goes round it. The building on the outside appears heavy, but that is owing to the order of architecture. The Duke of Argyle intends by degrees to remove the town of Inverary half a mile lower down Loch Fine, which now stands close to the castle. In the old house we saw the model of the new aedifice, with several other models of curious instruments etc. Amongst these was one of Marshall Saxe's travelling house, consisting of a drawing room 18 feet by 12 and a semicircular bedchamber 12 feet by 8 feet so ingeniously and mechanically contrived that the whole takes to pieces and when put up forms a waggon which 6 horses can draw. The Duke of Argyle built one from this model which cost £500, but was unfortunately blown over by the violence of the wind and destroyed.

The hills on every side are covered with forest trees and evergreens judiciously mixed. On the top of the highest is a tower in imitation of a ruin, from whence there is a delightfull view on every side. At the bottom is a small paddock with a few red deer, which is to be extended so as to comprehend that part of Glen Shira adjacent to Loch Fine. Here is a fresh water loch, which at high tides the sea flows into and brings salt-water fish, so that it frequently happens that salmon, salmon and fresh water trouts, herrings, haddock, mackrel and other sea and fresh water fish are caught promiscuously in the same net.

On the north is a kitchen garden of 6 acres, well planted. A mile southwest are two beautyfull hills covered with wood (the natural growth of the place) to the summit, which form at bottom the pleasant glen of Essachosaine, or Glen Love, which at the end has 2 cascades (one of these 40 feet high). The water of them forms a small rivulet which glides through the vale.

The people in this part of the world make hay with their hands and the Duke in the lands at a distance from the house is at no charge in making it, but when made takes a certain proportion (according to the distance) and gives them the residue. The land in this part sells at 35 years' purchase; herrings at Inverary sold 10 for a penny. The poor people have covered their chimneys with large stones to keep in the smoak. The method of buryal is here very remarkable amongst people of inferior rank, whose bodies when put into a coffin are carried by their neighbours on a ladder covered with plaid to the churchyard, where they dig a grave and throw them in without the ceremony of funeral service, which is not used in Scotland. The method of washing linnen is as comical as the other is barbarous. It is usual to see at the side of every river near a village the women, without shoes and stockings and their coats tucked up to their waists, treading the dirt out of the linen till the water is discoloured, when they put in fresh water and so continue treading until the linen is quite clean.

Beyond Inverary the military are making a new road to Teyendrom <Tyndrum>, which there is to fall in to the great road from Sterling to Fort William. They have already compleated 4 miles, which we passed in our way to Port Sonachan Ferry, 15 miles distant. The instant we left the new road we found ourselves in the most horrid paths that can be conceived, up and down steep hills, through bogs in some places, in others filled with large loose stones where our horses had no firm footing or, what was worse, now and then staircases of solid, craggy rock. In our way we were witnesses to a sight sufficient to shock human nature. At the door of a hut on the grass lay a child without anything to cover him but a waistcoat, his limbs stretched out and in all appearance stiff, without the least sign of life. Upon our calling to the woman of the house we found the small pox out upon it. I mention and reflect with horror at the savageness and inattention that the parents shewed upon this occasion.

Loch Aw (on which is Port Sonachan Ferry) is a fresh water lake 24 miles, with some few islands therein. The boat is extremely bad, covered with birch twigs at bottom (as indeed are all the boats in this country), capable of holding with safety not more than 2 horses at a time. The key from whence the horses embarked was made with loose stones, so that when they attempted to step into the boat, that giving way on one side and the stones on the other frightened the horses so much that it was very difficult to get them aboard. Add to this the stupidity of the Charon who was endowed with all the bad qualities of the ass and the mule.

9 miles of road equally barren and disagreable brought us to the kirk of Muckairn, where a miserable hut (that by selling rum had dignified itself with the appellation of a change-house) afforded us shelter, and that only; our horses we were obliged to graze in the field, whilst (like beggars when the toyl of day is over) we spread our wallets on the ground and regaled ourselves with provisions we had brought from Inverary. Not far from hence is a foundery for casting canon ball < Lorn Furnace, Bonawe >. It is upon Sir Duncan Campbell's estate and carryed on by Englishmen from Lancaster. 7½ miles more brought us to the Connel, on the banks of Loch Etyff < Etive >, where the tyde comes up from the sea and forms a very singular curiosity, a salt cascade.

2 miles southwest stands Dunstafnadge Castle, the oldest building in Scotland prior to Christianity. Here many Scotch kings lived and some Danish kings were buryed. It is now the residence of a gentleman of the name of Campbell. There is a very remarkable echo, the description of which I relate in Mr

Dunstaffnage Castle, Argyll. Engraved view after drawing by Francis Grose, c. 1789. (*Reproduced by permission of the RCAHMS*)

87

Dugalds Campbell's own words: "At Dunstafnadge stands an old chapel 50 feet long; the walls are 15 feet high. 30 yards distant from it is a perpendicular rock that runs parallel with the chapel, thought rather higher than the walls. If a person stands 100 yards behind this rock and speaks, or even whispers, the echo is heard in a very loud and distinct manner (as if coming from the chapel) by anyone who stands under the perpendicular rock on the opposite side to the speaker, and yet don't hear him speak one word, though he is 30 yards nearer them than the chapel is".

Having crossed the ferry at Loch Etyff < Etive >, 4½ miles would have brought us to Lochniel, the seat of Sir Duncan Campbell, but we were unfortunately benighted and lost our way in a place where we were surrounded on one side by impassable bogs, on the other by an arm of the sea into which we should probably have fallen had not chance sent an old woman to our assistance, who directed us to Sir Duncan's house after having wandered 2 miles out of the right road. Here we were received with the utmost hospitality, civility and politeness. The house < Lochnell House > is prettily situated on an eminence at a proper distance from the mountains and the sea, from which it is defended by a great variety of trees. The hills behind the house are planted in every part, which thrive extremely and are disposed with taste and judgement. Here I saw a single stalk of hemp 7 feet long and as thick as my wrist. Land sells here from 26 to 36 years' purchase and lets at 1d per acre moss, 2d pasture, arable 6d.

To Airds is 7½ miles. In our way we were obliged to pass Ruegarve < Rudha Garbh > Ferry, an arm of the sea where, having imprudently embarked with the horses and advanced halfway across, the water running rough, the Charons were frightened and suddenly turned the boat round (by which they endangered drowning us all by filling the boat with water) and rowed back to shore. Where being once more safely landed, I did not chuse to make another attempt in so much good company, so dispatched the horses first and followed after with no other brutes than the watermen. We reached Airds at dusk, where Mr Campbell of that place, and the rest of the family, received us with hospitality not inferior to his neighbour and to whom I think myself greatly indebted for their civilities. Here I found them making hay (their first crop) September 4th. The land sells here at 30 years' purchase and lets at 5s per acre. Labor from 6d to 8d per day. Manure, dung, seaweed, shell sand and lime. Shell sand is good for lands that never were tilled and excellent for moss land, on which if sprinkled even without plowing will make good pasture, but if plowed sufficiently, according to the roughness of the moss, will produce good crops without any other manure, the land first being properly drained. The soil upon the coast is chiefly sand and gravel, in some few places black mould and clay. The gentlemen of these parts are improving by drains unfathomable bogs, so that in 3 years' time they bear corn and soon become firm land.

About ½ mile from the shore lies the isle of Lismore, esteemed the richest soil in Scotland, being a fat, grey, marlish soil, which requires no other manure than to lay one ridge of the earth upon another. It is 8 miles long, 2 broad. The land is worth 10s per acre and sells at 30 years' purchase. There are the ruins of a castle <?Tirefour Broch> built by the Danes in a circular form on a hill close to the sea about 2 miles from the ferry. At Airds I saw (what I had searched Ireland for without effect) a wolf dog, which Mr Campbell was so obliging to give me. In these parts it is customary when a husband dies for the wife to have music the night before the buryal and begin a dance with her neighbours, and the relations of the deceased danced next according to their nearness of blood. This now prevails only amongst the lower class, though formerly was in use amongst people of high rank. It seems to me to bear a strong resemblance to the manners of the wild Indians.

From hence I intended to have made a vizit to Icolmkill

<Iona> (a place remarkable for being the first seminary of religion and learning in the country), but was prevented by the badness of the weather. I shall therefore transcribe the observations of a very ingenious man (versed in the antient languages), which he made on the spot. His name is John Campbell, a charity schoolmaster at Airds [10] in Argyleshire as follows. He was but 3 hours there and thinks he could have collected much more if he had not been interrupted.

"Icolmkill. March 5 1749. The remains of the buildings appear to have been the work of different ages and often repaired, with additions, since the days of St Colm, who resided there in the 6th century and crowned Aiden, the 49th king of the Scots. The church of St Mary, choir and steeple in the middle, with 2 isles or wings adjoined, resemble the figure of the cross. The steeple, 3 stories high, stands on 4 pretty arches adorned with work of low relief such as Adam and Eve in the state of innocence, the Devil tempting Eve, the Devil attending a man who steals his neighbor's cattle etc. 2 of the arches are 22 feet long, equal to the breadth of the church and choir within the walls, each of which is 60 feet long. The other 2 arches are about 16 feet long, the breadth of the isles adjoyning, each of which is 30 feet long, and the length of the whole building 144 feet over the walls. The steeple (which you ascend by a narrow winding stair of hewn stone) is almost entire and some of the roof timbers are seen. In the uppermost storey is a circular window, lozenged by arches of polished stone, meeting in the centre and forming an equal number of oblique spheric triangles so contrived as to admit abundance of light and exclude the wind and rain."

"The south wall of the church rises in very neat pillars wrought according to all the different orders of architecture, on which are cast arches, and in every arch a circular window as above, the whole admitting light to very near the height of the wall, except near the east end, where some low buildings had been joined and of which some ruins are seen. Joined to the north wall stood the buildings of the college, the common hall arched, the pend still entire and the area paved with hewn stone; galleries and seperate apartments for the students. North of these lie the ruins of the houses of the religious."

"Within the church on the northwest corner, by the wall lately built across, under the arch supporting the steeple on one side, is shewed an opening near the height of the side wall, into which they say St Colm retired at his stated hours of private devotion. By the wall on the east end, within the church, stands a piece of white marble 5 feet long, 5 feet broad, 2 inches thick (supposed to be the altar), very much broken at one corner by the country people, who imagine it to be a relict of St Colm and conclude it was an antidote for any disease in man or beast, and especially the flux."

"A little west of this, by the north side wall, is seen a grave stone of black marble, very fresh, supported by four pieces of freestone, rough hewn, each 1 foot high, on which in a fine *basso relievo* lyes Abbot MacFingone in his sacred habit, elbowing 2 lions at one end and spurning 2 at the other. And round the edge of the marble, in British characters, is this inscription: *+Hic +jacet +Johannes MacFingone abbas de Ii +qui obiit anno millesimo quingentesimo cujus anima propicietur altissimis. Amen.* Just opposite to this marble, by the south wall, is another monument of freestone, done after the same manner, for Abbot MacKenzie, but defaced."

"Within a small building close by the choir and joined to it on the south side, lyes interred Lachlan MacFingone, father to Abbot John, under a plain blueish stone with an inscription in the same characters, thus: *+Haec est crux Laclani MaicFingone et ejus filii Johannis abbatis de Ii facta anno domini MCCCCLXXXIX.* West of this, at a small distance, lyes a stone much impaired by time and to appearance more ancient than the former, with this inscription: *+Hic jacet Angusius filius Angusii MaicDomhuil domini de Isla.* Within a little stone enclosure on the north side, near the west end of the choir, is a grave stone, very much broke and in ruins, where the body of St Colm is supposed to be buried",(though Camden affirms <*Britannia* (1695), 1013.> his tomb to be at Downe, in the county of Downe in Ireland, according to an ancient distich inscribed on a tomb there: *Hi tres in duno tumulo tumulantur in uno/ Brigidia, Patricius atque Columba pius/*).

"A little north from thence is the statue of an abbot in his vestments, called by the people (who see nothing of the man's figure) in Irish N Tabbe Cammachassath, that is the crooked legged abbot. And near this +*Hic jacet Johannes Betonius Maclenorum familiae medicus qui obiit* . . . and below this distich: *Ecce cadit jaculo victrici mortis iniquae/ qui toties alios soluit ipse malis/.*"

"Fronting the church on the south side is the burying place of the chiefs of the clans, where lye several grave stones without any supporters, with a bas relief of men in armour upon them, but no inscription, said to belong to Macleod, MacQuarie and MacLean of Douart etc. West of these is the place of the tombs of the ancient kings of Scotland, whose places appear in rows, without any stone, monument or inscription above ground, except one very large stone on the east side, which appears to have had many letters cut upon it, yet none of them legible, and another whose edge is seen a little above ground with this ancient inscription, thus: < here follows an attempted facsimile of the letters > *Coromac Ulshada hic est situs*, that [is] Cormac barbatus. According to Dr Keting,[11] in his *Notitia Hiberniae*, Cormac Macart, one of the kings of Ireland, was buryed here AD 213."

"On the south side of the choir, a few paces west of the south isle, stands a cross of one solid stone, overgrown with fog, 14 feet 9 inches high, 1½ feet broad, 6 [inches] thick, fixed in a pedestal of one stone 2 feet high above ground, on which are hewn 3 stepes (like steps of a stair) quite round. A few paces south of this cross stands the walls of Rollic Ouran, or Ouran's chapel, 60 feet long, 22 feet broad. A small distance east from this chapel lyes a stone almost sunk under ground with an inscription of which only a few words can be seen thus: +*Hic jacent quatuor priores una* . . . South from St Mary's Church to the grand refectory, or nunnery, as they call it, for upwards of 300 paces, is a causeway in pretty good repair, crossed by another that leads to the shore and seems to have been made much after the same manner, though now it is decayed. On your right, as you go from the church to the nunnery, stands a cross 10 feet high, 14 inches broad, 3¾ inches thick, without any inscription or hieroglyphic."

"The remains of the nunnery appear grand even in ruin. The standing wall is near of an equal height all round, with an area that has been enclosed with a high wall and paved with hewn stone. In the east part of the fabric stands a spring arch entire and covers the whole breadth of the main building, but so decayed that the rain water drops through upon a black marble stone below, on which is a bas relief of a prioress in her vestments; above her head *Sancta maria ora pro me* and round the bas relief this inscription: +*Hic* +*jacet* +*domina Anna Donalda Terleti filia quondam priorissa de Iona quae obiit anno domini millesimo quingentesimo et undecimo cujus animam Abrahamo commendamus Amen. Here lyes Lady Anne Macdonald, Charles's daughter etc.* The whole appears majestic to the eye when first seen from the hills, rocks, bogs, moss and black mountains surrounded by the sea."

My companion having returned from Icolmkill on Saturday evening <?September 9th>, we set out the next morning for Fort William and about 2 miles from Airds saw a very large circular heap of stones called Cairnbane [12] in which are said to be several subterraneous apartments, the passages leading to them supported by large beams of timber in some places, in others by large stones; the entrance is now closed with a stone. What this could be intended for the inhabitants are at a loss to conjecture, unless it might be a receptacle for robbers, or in the former ages of barbarity afford a retreat to such who were desirous of avoiding the insults of their wild neighbours. 6 miles further brought us to an arm of the sea < Loch Leven >, where they were constrained to swim over the horses. On the other side we refreshed ourselves with provisions (our hospitable friend at Airds had accomodated us with) in a miserable hut in Lochaber, where the door and window performed each the double offices of lighting the house and furnishing an entrance and a vent for the smoke to evaporate at, and in a corner lay an infant full of the smallpox. In Glenrie < Gleann Righ >, about a mile from the place of baiting we passed a large waterfall, the noise of which is heard at a considerable distance. From this to the 3 mile water is a road that may fairly be termed a continued staircase, where our horses in some places were obliged to step down rocks 2 foot deep.

At Fort William the only thing to be seen is the fortification, strong neither by situation or art. Within 300 yards is a hill which commands the whole place, from whence the rebels assaulted and in all probability must easily have destroyed it had not drunkeness and a want of balls (of a proper weight for battering) prevented them. 1 mile northeast from hence is Ben Nevis, remarkable for being the highest hill in Britain (the ascent being 14 English miles) and in some parts always covered with snow, of which I was an eye witness. On the left hand, close to the road side, stands the ruins of the castle of Inverlochy, which vyes with that of Dunstafnage for antiquity; it is a square with a round tower at each corner.

A little farther brought us to Loch Lochy, 9 miles in length (formerly the estate of Lochiel), with the lands on the other side many miles up the country and where he had a good house < Achnacarry >, but having engaged in the last rebellion, burnt it himself to prevent the king's forces being benefited by it. The situation is extremely beautyful and romantic. It was placed on the edge of the lake; above it rises a hill covered with woods to a great extent and full of red deer. The estate being now vested in the Crown, the king's factor, Mr Mungo Campbell has built a little house there. The military road goes on the south side of the loch to a little village called Lagenadrom <Laggan>, the whole way through woods, with cascades almost every ten yards. Here I was forced to bait my horses with sheaves of corn and grass at the door of a hut which afforded nothing but whiskey and oat bread, so that I should have remained without refreshment had not Captain Barker (who commanded a party of soldiers in this place) very civily invited us to dine at his quarters, which was a hut that had been built at the expence of the government, for which 50 guineas was paid.

On the northeast side is another pleasant loch, called Loch Oich, which as we coasted we saw on the north the castle of Glengary <Invergarry Castle>, the property of Mcdonald of that place, who possesses £1000 per annum. It was burnt by the king's forces, since which the owner has contented himself with a hut close to it, where he resides. We passed by a copper mine on the south belonging to the same person, worked by a Jew of the name of Hart. It is at the top of a prodigious hill, the entrance to which is near the summit; it is not supposed to be very beneficial.

Fort Augustus is rather to be considered as a neat barrack than a fortification, being situated on the banks of Loch Ness and commanded on 3 sides. It consists of a small, well-contrived square with 4 circular bastions, in each of which is a circular tower; 2 of these are magazines for meal, 1 for gunpowder, the 4th a carpenter's shop. The governor's house and the other buildings make a good appearance; the whole of brick, has a dry ditch and a drawbridge at the entrance. We were politely entertained by Governor Trapaud, but were afterwards obliged to sleep in a miserable hut at Kilwhimen.

13 miles east is the famous cascade of Fieres <Foyers>, justly esteemed the finest in Britain, being a vast column of water which falls (from the River Strathereck) 30 yards perpendicularly amongst rocks with so great force that it ascends

again in mist to a considerable distance; from hence, after running half a mile it emptyes itself in Loch Ness. The rocks that surround it are extremely romantic, covered with shrubs from top to bottom. The whole belongs to Mr Frazer of Fieres, who has a house in the vale below it. 1 mile further stands a change house known by the title of Wade's Hut, that general having resided there when the troops made the roads after the rebellion in 1715. The expence and labour attending this work was surprizing, particularly at the passage of the red rock, where it is computed to have cost the government a guinea per foot. The road is remarkably pleasant to the end of the loch. It is a continued wood, through which, at the bottom, the water appears to great advantage.

The town of Inverness is situated almost at the mouth of the Ness, where it emptyes itself into the Firth of Murray <Moray>, a long, dirty, ill-built town remarkable for nothing but being the place that divides the north and south highlands. Here Cromwell is said to have settled a colony of English, and that language is thought to be spoke here in greater purity than any other part of Scotland. He built a small fort at the mouth of the river, of which the only remains are the raised mounds of earth. It is a seaport, though of small consequence, having but 2 manufactures of linen and plaid and probably will soon fall to decay when the new fort is compleated, which would have been placed at Inverness if the stupidity and irresolution of the merchants had not preventd it. On the south side of the town are the ruins of Fort George, which was blown up by the rebels in 1745. Its situation made it untenable against canon (being commanded by a rising ground in front) and like the other 2 forts must be rather intended as a checque upon the turbulency of its highland neighbours than expected to stand a siege. Arable lands lets from £0 2s 6d to £0 5s 0d per acre and sells at 30 years' purchase. Labor 6d per day.

From hence I took a view of Culloden Muir, made famous in the annals of this country for the defeat of the rebel forces in 1745, for an accurate description of which I must refer you to the histories of that time. Adjoining to the place where the battle was fought is the house of Mr Forbes < Culloden House >, an antique irregular aedifice surrounded on every side with thick groves of fir. The famous Duncan Forbes, Lord President of the Court of Session, held it out against the Pretender for some time, a man no less to be admired for his integrity and great abilities in his judicial capacity than his loyalty and unwearied attention to the public service in that critical conjuncture. His countrymen and fellow students have in testimony of their esteem erected a statue (in the Parliament House at Edinburgh) to perpetuate the memory of his services.

12 miles east lyes the new fort, to which we coasted on the side of the firth and in our way passed by an old uninhabited house of Lord Murray's < Moray's > called Castle Stuart. The roads in this neighbourhood are remarkably good and the country fertile. About a mile and a half from the fort we crossed the military road that leads to Bremar. Fort George is situated at the end of a long point of land which runs far into the Firth of Murray and commands the entrance (called Ardesir Point). It is of a very irregular form (contrived by Colonel Skinner, under whose direction it is carryed on) calculated to suit the point of land. The particulars are as follows < the following notes were probably intended to refer to a sketch or plan of the fort which has not survived >: 4 bastions and 2 demy bastions. A Pr[ince] of W[ales's bastion], B D[uke] of C[umberland's bastion], C Pr[ince] H[enry] W[illia]m['s bastion], D P[rince] H[enry] Fr[ederick's bastion], E 2 casemates or barracks in the curtain, bombproof; the 2 casemates are on each side the angle between the 2 demy bastions and there is a magazine in the middle to supply them, F a grand magazine, G barracks, H main ditch to be filled to the depth of 6 feet, I 2 sluices to fill the main ditch and fosse round the ravelin, K guard house in the ravelin, L ravelin, M fosse round the ravelin, N 2 lunets, O the covered way, P bridge guard, Q principal barrier, R barrier.

The situation north and south. The first entrance faces the south, from whence you enter the ravelin by a drawbridge over the fosse. Thence to the grand entrance (which is to the east) by another drawbridge across the main ditch, which when passed you go through an archway, on the right and left of which are to be the houses of the governor and lieutenant governor, fronting the entrance to a great square 120 yards long, 22½ broad, where are noble barracks capable of containing 3 regiments. There are no outworks, except to the land side. The ground round the fortification is shingles entirely, and that it may not be commanded from any part the government intend to remove the only hill (which is at a distance of ½ a mile) when the works are compleated, for which £10,000 is annually given by Parliament; and when perfected it is thought will be the strongest in Britain. The method of making a place bomb-proof is as follows. When the arch is turned they cover it with a composition of mortar or cement mixed with oyl to prevent rain penetrating through. Over this is placed: 1 a layer stones, 2 ditto of clay, 3 ditto of earth, and so alternately, each well rammed down. On the northwest they intend to run out a pier and make a safe harbor for ships, the firth there forming itself into a bay.

7½ miles along the coast brought us to Nairn, a poor, mean town though the chief of the county of that name. Near Nairn we had a good view of Cromarty Bay, esteemed the largest in Britain, being 18 miles round. And 12 miles to Logie, where we were hospitably received and agreably entertained by Mr Tulloch, who has a small house <?Logie House> seated at the foot of a moor on the banks of the River Findhorn. Land here sells at 30 years' purchase, lets from 20s to 22s per Scots acre. A sandy soil, very improveable by turnips. Harvest labor 6d and victuals, common ditto 6d, mowing 1s and victuals. Manure, dung and lime. 1 mile north is Tarnaway <Darnaway> Castle, another uninhabited house of Lord Murray's <Moray's>. 3 mile east lies Moy, a small, old house belonging to Sir Ludovick Grant in a fine country with a good view of the town of Forres in front.

18 miles north <south> of Logie, in the highlands, stands Castle Grant, another seat of Sir Ludovick Grant. The road is good, being made at Sir Ludovick's expence. In our way we passed by a pleasant, romantic vale filled with wood, in the midst of which, on a small hill, are the ruins of an old castle <?Dunphail> (the property of the same gentleman). The castle of Grant is seated on an eminence in the midst of wild hills, which the owner has endeavoured to make as agreable to the eye as possible by planting those immediately adjacent to the house with firs.

2 miles south is the bridge of Spey, over the river of that name, consisting of 3 arches very remarkably large, 6 miles west of which are the woods of Abernethy belonging (as indeed the whole country does) to Sir Ludovick Grant. They are the most extensive I have seen, one of them being 18 miles, another 15 miles in circumference, all fir and the natural growth. The smallest of these was set on fire by some people who wanted to lower <?raise> the price of wood and took that opportunity of putting their design in execution and alledged it was done by the rebels. A person employed by Sir Ludovick Grant numbered the trees destroyed from 50 to 100 years' growth, which he assured me amounted to 2,464,160. They fell great quantities of this timber annually and after cutting off the branches etc bring the bodies of the trees to a saw mill, whence after being sawed into boards they convey them to the Spey side and thence float them on rafts down the river when the water is high.

The vale called the strath of Spey is a most fertile spot, which extends several miles up the country. On its banks we saw several large herds of cattle feeding, by which the inhabitants are considerable gainers. At particular times it overflows and enriches the country, not like the other streams and rivers, which cover the land with stones brought down by the violence of the current; the bottom is a hard sand. The land here sells from 20 to 50 years' purchase; best arable lets at 5s per acre. The manure is dung and lime. Labor 6d, woodcutters £0 1s 0d per day. We afterwards rode up the vale of Glencarney, another rich, fertile strath producing barley and oats and pasture. Sir Ludovick Grant is making a detached road to join the king's road leading from Bremar to that which comes from Delnachardich <Dalnacardoch> and by that means open a new communication for several miles, a work that will be highly serviceable to travellers and for which the person at whose expence it is done justly merits the thanks of the public.

The 21st <September> we returned to Moy 21 miles distant from Castle Grant. 23rd we went to view the ruins of the abbey of Kinloss, consisting of a neat arch or gateway, several pillars that supported a small room, the side wall of the cloister and 2 old houses, one with a coat of arms over the door having 3 crosses and behind the coat a crosier; this was inhabited by a farmer. The other had likewise a coat of arms over the door on which is a deer, or goat's, head and a crosier as the first. The family here consisted of rooks and jackdaws.

On our entrance to the town of Forres stands a flat square pillar <Sueno's Stone> said to be 23 feet above and 12 feet underground, the breadth 3 feet 2 inches at the bottom. It is surounded by steps to support it at Lady Murray's <Moray's> expence. The upper part is much defaced and broke. On one side is represented many hieroglyphical figures, amongst which are beasts with human heads. On the other a cross, beneath it 2 human figures of a much larger form than any of the rest. The other parts are filled with mosaic work and the edges are filled with scroll work. The whole consists of 7 compartments. Camden says <*Britannia* (1695), 955> this was erected in memory of a victory obtained by King Malcolm MacKenneth over Sweno, King of Denmark and I am induced to be so far of his opinion that it was intended to be a monument of some victory which the Scots gained over an invader, because in those early ages it was usual on such occasions for the conquorers to describe their enemies under monstrous forms, by which they magnifyed their own bravery and skill in overcoming them and raised themselves to a higher pitch of esteem in the opinions of their countreymen.

At the north side are the remains of Macbeth's castle [13] . . . <two lines of text partially obliterated> . . . the lower part is still to be seen entire. It appears to have been a small building placed on a rising ground commanding a good prospect of the flat county adjacent. It is the property of Sir William Dunbar, who has made a small garden at one side, but having retired to another part of the highlands it lies open to the public. The town consists of one long, ill-built street, enjoys a market and with some others the right of sending a member to Parliament, but I fear is not in a very thriving condition, being filled with beggars from one end to the other. In these parts you can rarely go from one village or town to another without passing a river, which is always inconvenient, sometimes dangerous. The country here is extremely good, chiefly arable, scarce any pasture. In some places I passed large commons which might afford grass to great quantities of sheep, if the poor did not take away turf to cover their huts, by which these waste lands are entirely bereaved of the green sward.

1½ miles north of Moy is Brodie, the seat of Mr Brodie, in great repute for its fine walks and plantations. I can't say they are disposed with taste, being in some places cut into arbors and other whimsical shapes, from which you see nothing. The great walks are indeed well contrived, each of them being terminated by some agreable object at a distance. The present owner is a minor, which affords an apology for their gardens not being kept in order. 13 miles brought us to Elgin, through good roads and a fertile country. The town consists of one good street. The houses are built on piazzas, which contribute much to gain a traveller's opinion in favour of them. At the north <west> end are the ruins of an old castle <Elgin

Castle >; at the south < east > the remains of the abbey < cathedral > (which are very large). It stands east and west. The east window is entire, between 2 square towers. The west window deficient only at the point; on each side is an octagon conical tower. The nave is too narrow; one transept, on the south part of which are 2 tombs with figures of men in armour. On the north is the chapter house supported by one pillar in the middle.

Travelling 9 miles we came to the River Spey, which we passed at the same part nearly where the Duke's army crossed 1745 and could not help being surprized at the infatuation of the rebels in not attempting to obstruct the passage of our own troops (as John Roy Stuart [14] advised), which if they had done, would have been rendered extremely hazardous. On the opposite side is the village of Faucuburs < Fochabers >, a poor, miserable collection, or rather cluster, of huts remarkable for the Duke of Gordon's seat (Castle Gordon) adjoyning to it, 1 part consisting of an old castle, the other of a modern building tacked to it. What the inside is I am at a loss to say, not being able to get admission as the porter was out. It is seated in a bad, moorish country, to cover which there are made large plantations of fir. The whole is sadly neglected, particularly the garden, which is sowed with corn in the front of the house.

12 miles distant is Cullen, a paultry, mean town belonging to Lord Finlater, who to encourge industry and set the poor to work has lent £2000 without interest to different persons towards carrying on manufactorys, who are to pay £50 yearly till the principal is repaid. The utility of this has already appeared by the working 2 manufactories of linen, each 14 looms, 1 stocking ditto intending to have 11 looms, 5 of which are already worked. There is a mill for throwing or twisting thread and a bleaching mill for linen. Land here sells from 32 to 35 years' purchase and lets at £0 10s 0d per acre. Labor 5d per day. On the point of a rock stands Lord Finlater's castle < Cullen House > (on the other side enclosed by the town) from which to the opposite hill they have been obliged [to] throw

Elgin Cathe-
dral,
Morayshire. En-
graved view by
Thomas,
c.1791. *(Repro-*
duced by
permission of
RCAHMS)

103

a bridge in order to have a communication. The arch is 60 feet high, 82 feet wide. A mile more south is Portsoy, the property of the same person, who from a single house has within the compass of a few years raised it to a large village said to contain 1000 inhabitants, who drive a good trade in corn.

Bamf is 12 miles from Cullen, a small town tolerably well built, has 3 linen manufactorys, a port to which belong 12 sail of ships from 40 to 100 tons burthen. From hence they export annually 10,000 boll of corn and oatmeal (8 stone to the boll). At the foot of the town flows the Devron, the royalty of which belongs to Lord Braco, who lets the salmon fishery there for £800, and other advantages amounting to £200 more per annum. This produces annually 60 last of salmon (12 barrel to the last), which they send to the Mediterranean. They export, moreover, linen yarn to London. Land sells from 38 to 40 years' purchase, lets in the country at 5s per acre, but some pasture round the town pays Mr Duff £7 per acre. Labor in winter 4d, in summer 6d per day; gardiners ditto 10d. Manure, dung, lime, seaweed and shells. On a hill close to the sea stands the castle of Bamf, formerly the property of the Earls of Buchan, but now belonging to Lord Deskford.

On the other side of the town, in a pleasant valley, is Duff House, the seat of Mr Duff, Lord Braco's eldest son. It is a magnificent aedifice consisting of 4 fronts; the grand entrance is to the west. At each corner is a square tower, which at the top appears heavy. The only part finished is a few rooms in the attic story; the saloon is a cube of 30 feet. In the north and south fronts, on each side the great windows, are placed several small windows, which give light to closets, but on the outside are very displeasing to the eye. The inside when finished will be extremely convenient. The plain on which the house stands is extensive, flanked towards the southeast by the River Devron, on the banks of which is a terrce 30 feet wide and one mile long, the opposite side and the neighbouring hills planted with forest trees and evergreens. In the river is a small island containing a kitchen and dineing room over it. Bamf is remarkable for fine weather. The number of inhabitants are 2000 and the corporation presented us with our freedom.

From hence we went 9 miles to Turrif, mostly over a disagreable country covered with heath, which continues quite to Old Meldrum and thence to Aberdeen, with the intervention of a few spots of corn ground. At Old Aberdeen we passed the Don over a bridge of one beautyfull Gothic arch remarkably large, and a little farther a good house <Seaton House> belonging to Mr Middleton seated in a pleasant vale. Here are the remains of the cathedral converted to a kirk, and the college or university founded by Bishop Elphinstone, in which is a good chapel never used for divine service, a library, schools and 10 professors. The scholars here wear a uniform dress, live in the college and dine regularly in the hall (contrary to the practice of most of the Scotch universities), where there are 2 tables, at which 4 of the professors attend alternately to see the students are properly provided with victuals. Those scholars who set at the first pay £2 15s 0d per quarter for commons, those of the 2nd table £2 0s 0d. This college is seldom full, occasioned by its being so near that of New Aberdeen, where the terms are shorter and the students reside in the town, which makes the expences of education less. This college was founded by one of the Keith family and is called Marishal College. It is a mean, paultry building.

New Aberdeen is a well-built town of large extent, in which [is] the best town hall in Scotland; a school; 4 hospitals and an infirmary viz. 1 Gordon's, for boys, £600 per annum, 2 Burghers' Hospital for decayed merchants, 3 Trinity ditto for tradesmen, 4 Drum's ditto for old women; a handsome new church <St Nicholas> built by Adams <James Gibbs> and joined to another very antique; and an English chapel. On the northwest side of the town they are makeing a walk ¼ of a mile in length, a canal on the side of it and beyond that a bleaching field. The society of freemasons have erected a handsome inn and therein a spatious room for a lodge. 2 miles from the town is a bleaching mill to whiten and wash linen. At the east end is a hill where formerly stood a castle. Here is a port to which belong 30 sail from 30 to 300 tons. Here is the manufactory of stockings all knit, none wove. The chief exports are stockings, linen and serge to the amount of £80,000 and about 1200 barrels of salmon, some yarn to London. The imports are flax, hemp and grocery from London. Trade is now on the decline. Land sells from 30 to 40 years' purchase; lets about the town from £3 0s 0d to £5 0s 0d per acre. Labor 7d per day. Number of inhabitants between 12,000 and 14,000.

A mile from the town we passed the Dee, over a stately stone bridge of 7 arches, and having rode 18 miles came to Stonehive < Stonehaven >, a poor fishing town seated in a small bay close to the seaside. At a small distance from hence to the south are to be seen the ruins of Dunotyr Castle, once a place of great strength. It stands on the summit of a steep rock that runs out into the sea, the access to which is extremely difficult, there being only one entrance and that so narrow as not to admit more than 2 persons abreast. It is in several places bombproof, but is commanded by a hill on the north side. It formerly belonged to the family of Keith, Earls of Marishal, whose estate was forfeited in 1715. From hence we passed through a fertile country 12 miles to Bervy < Inverbervie >, another small town on the seaside. Here I saw a second crop of clover and rye grass getting in September 31st < sic >. There is no manner of trade stirring in this village. They have indeed 4 looms for weaving sail cloth (which are employed by the factory at Montrose) and a small bleaching mill for thread.

From Bervy we had an exceeding pleasant journey over a fertile country of 12 miles to Montrose with a view of the sea the whole way. Montrose is a large, neat, well-built town consisting of one principal street. It has a fine harbor capable of containing ships of great burthen. To this port belong 50 sail of ships from 20 to 200 tons and was once more considerable, but having suffered greatly in the last Spanish War has not yet recovered its pristine strength. The annual exports from hence are 700 barrels, or 60 last, of salmon, sailcloth to the amount of £20,000, brown linen and osnabrugs £40,000 and 20,000 pound weight of thread, of which there are two manufactories. Imports, deals and about 300 ton of flax from Riga and Narva, together wth all sorts of London goods. There are 2 rope walks. The number of inhabitants are computed at 6000. Land sells from 25 to 30 years' purchase. Arable land where the soil is clay and near the town lets at from £1 10s 0d to £2 10s 0d per acre. The price of labor is intolerably dear, being 8d per day, which for common labourers is higher than almost any other part of Scotland. Before I take my leave of this pleasant spot I must do justice to the English chapel, built and maintained by voluntary subscription, which for neatness exceeds every one I have seen in Scotland.

The country from hence to Brechin is good, producing great quantities of grain. Brechin was once a bishop's see. The town is tolerably well built and now noted only for its cattle market and salmon fishery. The round steeple here is very remarkable; it is in some measure detached from the main body of the church. Its height from base to cornice is 85 feet, thence to the vane 15 feet, external circumference 47 feet, wall 3 feet 8 inches thick; it consists of 60 regular courses of hewn stone. The door is to the south. The castle < Brechin Castle > is on the south side of the town on a rising ground which commands a fine view of the adjacent country. The gardens are well disposed; a terrace surrounds the house and at the foot of the hill flows the River South Esk, over which there is a stone bridge consisting of 2 arches. The house belongs to Lord Panmure, but is quite unfurnished, having been plundered by the rebels in 1745. Here the late Lord Panmure entertained the Pretender 1715 and went to the Battle of Sheriffmuir, for which the estate and title was forfeited, but the estate restored to the present owner and the same titles conferred on him in Ireland.

4 miles south from Brechin, at Aberlemny, in a field adjoyning to the road and fixed in the ground close to a stone wall, we saw 2 large stones about 10 feet high. The first of these was entirely defaced on one side; the other was filled [with] rude figures of men on horseback. The 2nd has on one side a cross, at the bottom of which on each side are 2 human figures in an inclined posture. On the other side are bows and arrows, men on horseback represented flying away and behind them dogs. What they were intended for I could not learn, but should suppose them to be monuments of some victory obtained over the Danes. Gordon says <*Itinerarium Septentrionale* (1726)> they were monuments of victories over the Danes *vide* p. 152.

Travelling through an indifferent country 12 miles we came to Forfar, a mean, ill-built town which carryes on a large trade in brown linens with Dundee, having 80 masters of looms. They make likewise here brogues for the highlanders. Land sell[s] at 25 years purchase, arable lets from £0 16s 8d to £1 10 0 per acre. Price of labor in harvest, men 6d, women 5d, other common labor 4d and victuals. Close to the town is a large loch of the same name. 4½ miles is Glames, the seat of Lord Strathmore. In the churchyard stands King Malcolm's gravestone, said to be 16 feet high and 5 feet broad by Gordon <*Itinerarium Septentrionale* (1726), 162>; only 8 or 9 feet now appears above ground. On one side is a cross filled with mosaic work, at the bottom of which is a king and the 2 murtherers, one of them with a pickax on his shoulder. On the other side are rudely engraved a fish and an eel to denote Loch Forfar, where the assassins were drowned endeavouring to escape, in memory of which murder of Malcolm 2nd this was erected.

At Miggle <Meigle>, 6 miles southwest of Glamis, in the churchyard we saw a flat stone standing upright 6 feet 1 inch high, 3 feet 4 inches broad. On one side is a cross filled with the figures of wild beasts; on the reverse 3 men on horseback, a woman between 2 lyons who try to devour her, a deer's head on another animal's body; at bottom 2 bears. Another stone 5 feet 6 inches high, 3 feet 3 inches broad; on one side a cross with mosaic work; reverse a salmon, a unicorn's head, a serpent and a man on horseback. A broken pillar sunk in the ground rising above the surface 3 feet 6 inches in height, the width 1 foot 10 inches. On one part are 2 men on horseback and several other figures so defaced that we could not make them out. By a hollow on the top there appears to have been something fixed there. Between the two large stones lye 3 small fragments. On the 1st is represented a person drawn in a chain with one horse, with a 2nd person sitting before and driving and a beast tearing a man; in another part a man armed with a bow and arrows and shooting at a beast. On the 2nd are 3 small crosses with leopards and dogs between them. The 3rd is filled with flowers. Near Miggle < at Belmont > we were shewed a small mount where McDuff killed Macbeth, who is supposed to be buryed there; it is called Bally Duff – Bellum Duffi.

The castle of Glamis is esteemed one of the finest and largest old palaces in Scotland; it has been finished at different times. The staircase was designed by Inigo Jones and is extremely beautyfull. The avenue that leads to the front of the house exceeds half an English mile. The country in which it stands is called the Vale of Strathmore; it is one of the richest and best cultivated in Scotland. The lands in some part of it are enclosed with quick hedges, which produce a good effect. Land near Glamis [sells] from 23 to 40 years' purchase; lets from £0 10s 0d to £1 0s 0d per acre. Labor from 6d to 8d.

Saturday October 9th I went to Castle Lyon < Castle Huntly >, another seat of the Strathmore family and built by Earl Patrick in the last century, who intended to have built 2 wings, but dyeing before the plan was executed the design has never been compleated, so that there is only the body of the house, situated on a rock at the borders of the Carse of Gowry, over which (together with the Firth of Tay and the opposite shore) it commands a good prospect. The entrances to the castle

Glamis Castle, Angus. Engraved view after drawing by James Moore, c. 1792. (*Reproduced by permission of the RCAHMS*)

are three, north, south and west. The first is the chief approach, which has no less than 7 arches or courts through which you must pass before you arrive at your journey's end, absurdities so glaring that every passenger must reflect on his Lordship's bad taste. The house is large and well contrived to receive a numerous family, but is now entirely uninhabited, the last dowager having carried away all the furniture.

6 long miles through a low country brought me to Errol, a poor, dirty town situated on a rising ground which Mr Crawford (who lives close to it) has improved with large plantations. From his house <Errol> and garden you may see the Carse, the Tay and the coast of Fife to the utmost advantage. Almost opposite stands an old castle belonging to Lord Rothes <Ballinbreich>. The lands here are worth 35 years' purchase; [let] from £1 10s 0d to £2 0s 0d per acre. The soil is a strong clay which continues almost through the whole Carse and renders the lands of a value nearly equal. In the garden I saw 2 trees of *arbor vitae* of prodigious size, so that I might say they were fit for timber, which in this sort of tree is very uncommon. The Carse of Gowry is esteemed the finest part of Scotland and I think with great reason. The lands are well cultivated and produce large quantities of grain. The road from Castle Lyon to Glamis is rather disagreable; the lands covered with heath wear an appearance which bears a strong resemblance to the highlands.

18 miles southeast of Glamis lies Aberbrothic <Arbroath>, a very long town close to the seaside consisting of 1 large street. It has a harbor to which belong 12 sail of ships trading to Riga for flax and timber. Its manufactures are cheques, osnabrugs, diaper, bleached yarn and thread. At the north entrance are the ruins of a large abbey built of reddish stone. The west door is a small, sharp, pointed arch, immediately over which on the outside are 3 arches of the same sort and above that the remains of a Catherine wheel window. On each side the door is a large, square tower to terminate the isles. That towards the north is

most entire, in which are 2 long, narrow, pointed windows; below these an arcade of 4 whole arches and underneath another consisting of 3 whole and 2 half arches partly sunk in the ground. Above the door on the inside is an open arcade of 6 arches. Each tower consists of one beautyfull large pointed ditto. At bottom in the next storey an arcade of 2 ditto in a circular arch. In the north side of the north tower 2 long, narrow windows and just without the tower, at the entrance to the isle, a door of the same sort.

There has been only one transept, of which the south part only remains, consisting of storeys: 1 a circular window, 2 two long, narrow, pointed ditto, 3 a gallery of 7 round arches, 4 an arcade of 8 pointed arches, 5 a circular door and 6 < here there is a drawing of a trefoil arch > ditto. On the west side of this transept 2 prodigious, long, narrow windows and below an arcade of 10 arches. Divided from this by a narrow wall is a square building in which are 3 small repositorys for bones. I endeavoured to take the dimensions, but was prevented from doing it exactly by the unevenness of the ground, so that you must make allowance for that. The length from the west to the east end is 180 feet, ditto of the cross 108 feet; bredth of the isles 45 feet. Joined to the church by a long building is a spatious gateway entire, consisting of 2 outward circular arches and in the middle within 1 pointed with a small [?one] on one side. The length of this gateway is 57 feet; bredth 12 feet. The country round the town is good, but the rest of the way very indifferent.

From hence we went 7½ miles to Panmure, the seat of Lord Panmure. The house was built at the beginning of the last century and is remarkably regular for that time of day. The extensive plantations which surround it are disposed with great judgement. From hence there is [a] good view of the sea, the coast of Fife and at a great distance that of Lothian, but the land between the house and the ocean detracts much from the pleasantness of the prospect, being barren and wet. The plantations consist chiefly of fir and beech, the latter immediately adjacent to the house and in greater quantity than I have seen at any other place.

12 miles brought us back to Glamis well pleased with everything that we had seen, except one, which was the hills at a distance covered with snow, October 13th, and which we were assured would not be melted till next June. The frosts at Glamis are now as severe as we usually experience them in England the latter end of November. October 16th < ?sic > I went to see Denoon Castle, 1 mile south west from Glamis, seated on an eminence environed on one side with a steep rock and rendered on all sides very difficult of ascent; on the north are 2 or 3 rows of terraces. It is of an irregular form, being in three parts semicircular and makeing nearly a straight line in the 4th. The walls are stone (covered with earth), which may be traced in several parts. Height 27 feet; thickness 30 feet; the whole circumference 330 English yards. It has 2 entries, 1 southeast another northwest. Within the tracks of buildings are visible.

Saturday 14th [October] I left Glamis and having rode through a very disagreable country 12 miles together arrived at Dundee, a town of extensive trade seated on the banks (and not far from the mouth) of the Firth of Tay. Its manufactures are brown and white linens, the exports of which annually amount to £45,000 nearby, Dundee thread, tallow and other commodities, £3,000. Imports, 200 last of flax from Narva and Riga, iron and timber from Sweden, English goods from London. The lands immediately adjacent to the town are very fertile and sell from 30 to 34 years' purchase. Pasture lets from £3 to £4, arable from £1 0s 0d to £1 10s 0d per acre. Labor is from 6d to 8d per day. The shipping belonging to the port amount to £20,000. Here is a handsome town hall and a good old tower to the kirk, which is spoiled by a building placed at the top. The number of inhabitants exceed 10,000.

Having crossed the Tay to the opposite coast of Fife I went ten miles and a half to St Andrews through a pleasant country and at a village < Leuchars > about 3 miles from thence saw the remains of part of a church remarkable for its antiquity, a circular building consisting of 2 rows of arches, those in the upper part 5 and round, in the lower of the same sort intersecting each other. The north part entire, the south part much decayed. At the east end of this building is a semicircular projection with 2 circular rows of arches the same at bottom as at top.

At St Andrews we saw with regret the ruins of many different buildings, which bore sufficient testimony of its pristine grandeur. The town formerly consisted of 4 grand streets going almost parallell to one another from east to west, all of them terminateing eastward at the cathedral. St Salvator's College was founded by Kennedy, Bishop of St Andrews, 1448. The chapel remains intire and is a venerable piece of antiquity. The roof is vaulted, without ornaments, not one pillar to be seen either in the middle or sides; the east end is a regular semicircle, the windows all pointed. The length is 111 feet, bredth 27. On the north side Bishop Kennedy has a stately monument of Gothic architecture with several niches where statues have once stood. At the entrance is a monument to Mr Pitcairne, 1695, and on the opposite side another to Mr Home with the following inscription: *MEMORIAE / OPTIMAE SPEI ADOLESCENTIS / JOHANNIS HOME / JACOBI HOME A BLACADER EQUITIS / FILII NATU MAJORIS / QUI DUM ARTIBUS LIBERALIBUS / IN ACADEMIA ANDREANA / SUMMA CUM LAUDE OPERAM NAVERAT / TABE CONFECTUS VITA DECESSIT / HOC MONUMENTUM PARENTES MAESTI / SACRUM ESSE VOLUERUNT /.* Underneath: *JACOBO HOME A BLACADER EQUITI / QUI FILIO PARUM SUPERVIXIT / UXOR PONI CURAVIT /.*

The college is partly new built, but not compleated for want of money to defray the expence. The library is a handsome room commanding a pleasant view of the sea. The other side are in ruins. St Leonard's College was founded in the reign of James 5th by John Hepburne, prior of St Andrews, the new college < St Mary's > by Archbishop Bethune. In a room where the schools are now kept Charles 1st held a parliament. By an act passed 20 George 2 these two colleges are united.

On the north side of the town are to be seen the walls of the old castle built by Roger, Bishop of St Andrews, who died 1202, to the east of which are the ruins of the cathedral, founded by Bishop Arnold, who died 1163, and finished by Roger, Bishop of St Andrews, who died 1328. Its length from east to west 370 feet, the cross from south to north 180 feet, its height 100 feet. The west entrance is by a large, pointed arch highly ornamented, above which is a close arcade of 7 trefoiled pointed arches. In the 3rd story 2 large arches pointed, with windows, one of which is entire; above this was another story quite lost. On each side of the door was a turret, the north invisible, the south entire, octagon, with 8 semicircular windows. Adjoining to the lower part of the turret on the right hand an arcade of 4 arches; under them, half sunk in the ground, another of 5. The wall of the south isle is standing; it is 17 feet wide. In it are 12 large arches, 8 pointed, 4 semicircular, at the west end of which is one pointed arch containing a small, close, circular ditto. From the springing of the arches the nave appears to have been divided from the isles by 2 rows of pillars forming a colonnade above each other, the highest very small. The west wall of the south transept only remains, containing 3 semicircular windows. On the sides of the middle window are 2 flat, semicircular arches against the wall and one on the outermost side; underneath an arcade of 10 semicircular arches intersecting each other. The east end of the nave almost entire; at bottom 3 high semicircular windows, above these a larger ditto in pointed arch. On each side a tower with octagon spires.

Behind the cathedral are the walls of St Rule's Chapel with the great square spire still entire; its height is 105 feet. In Trinity Church is a superb monument to Archbishop Sharp, with the particulars of his murder and the figures of the assassins in *alto relievo*. Sir William Sharp (who erected it), the Archbishop's son, left 6000 merks to the city of St Andrews to keep it in repair, which I wish had the intended effect, for [on] one side the coat of arms, ditto on the other and mitre, are fallen off without being replaced, though the present mayor <provost> I was told is a descendant of the family. The haven is so ruinous and decayed that it had only one ship belonging to it, which is taken.

From hence to Elly <Elie> we passed through a fertile country abounding with coal and were hospitably entertained by Captain Keyd, who has fitted up a a neat box close to the seashore in the English taste. The lands in this parish are the property of Sir John Anstruther, who has a good old house <Elie House> defended from the sea by extensive plantations. The soil is sand for near 2 feet and then is succeeded by a stiff clay; this is daily improved by turnips and by degrees made to bear good grass. The manure is dung, lime and seaweed. When the latter is laid upon the lands, and they plowed up, the salts of it are so serviceble that the farmer has a crop of barley every year without being obliged to let it lye fallow. The price of land is from 25 to 35 years' purchase. Arable, when very good, lets at 20s per acre, open pasture at 10s, enclosed ditto at £1 5s 0d. Labor 6d per day.

In a small bay within Sir John Anstruther's land red stones resembling rubies in color and hardness are continually washed up by the sea from amongst the rocks. They are generally very small, but sometimes are found of the size of a pea. They likewise find them (by breaking the rocks) sometimes a foot deep within them, often sticking to the outside. It is remarkable that these stones are never met with on any other part of the coast, except this little spot. Large shoals of herring once frequented this coast, but have now forsaken it.

Monday 16th <October> we travelled 19½ miles through a fruitfull country abounding in corn and coal to Kinghorne and in the way thither passed through Dysert, a miserable sea village and another long town much better built called

Burntisland. Kinghorne is a dirty place of no considerable trade, known only by being the station of the ordinary passage boats to and from Leith. The Forth at this place is called 7 miles wide, but it is generally made 10½ miles by the necessity of tacking 2 or 3 times, which lengthened our pasage to 2 hours and half. The harbour at Kinghorne is bad at present, but it probably will not long continue so, as they are carrying out the pier to a considerable distance. The boats are extremely good, very justly esteemed the best in Scotland, and the people who navigate them sober and skillfull, so that no boat was ever known to be lost at this ferry though they pass every day and in all weathers.

Leith is a very populous town, the port from whence the trade of all that part of Scotland is carryed on. I was unable to inform myself of particulars, not remaining there half an hour. The key is extremely fine. From thence to our lodgings in Edinburgh was 3 miles, where staying one night we set forward on Tuesday 17<th October> for Roslin, 7½ miles southwest from Edinburgh, where are the ruins of a castle, once the dwelling-place of the Lords Sinclair, in a most delightfull and romantic situation. And at a little distance from it stands Roslin Chapel, entire, the property of General Sinclair, who keeps it glazed and in the best repair, a proceeding which will always do him honour and procure him esteem in the opinion of every good man and admirer of antiquity.

This beautyfull building is 57 feet long, 27 broad; the 2 isles are 6 feet each broad. It is not in the shape of a cross, but like our common chappels and has no transept. The cieling is coved, with fine workmanship, divided into 5 compartments, each highly ornamented with different sorts of flours carved in stone, as indeed the whole is throughout. On each side 5 pointed windows, the work of the arches rather plain, between which are 4 niches on each side, as likewise 2 at the east and 2 at the west end, where statues of the 12 apostles are supposed to have stood. At the east end is a large pointed arch ornamented richly at the top and sides. Under the window at the east end are 2 rows of pointed arches much adorned with scripture, history and flowers. One of the pillars that support these arches is fluted and wreathed. At the west part of the chappel is a monument of Lord Caithness, 1582. On the outside are 6 perpendicular buttresses with niches in the middle of each, on the upper part of which are elegant small turrets, all of different sorts; the upper part of these resemble Henry 7 chappel at Canterbury <?Westminster> in workmanship. On the east side 5 ditto. The window on the outside is neat and elegant. On the north are 7 buttresses of the same make and each hath a small turret, but they differ from each other.

At Newbottle, 7½ miles from Roslin, are many curious old portraits, amongst which are: 1 *Buchanan*; 2 *Sir Philip Sydney* in his armour, half length, good color and expression; 3 *Sir Francis Drake, Sir Walter Raleigh and another figure* in one picture; Sir Francis leans on a globe and points at the way he went round the world. In a gallery 54 feet long, 30 broad, crowded with portraits are 1 *Henry 8* by H Holbein, extremely fine; 6 Lelys; 7th *James 1* full length, very good; 8 *A Piece of Architecture*; several of the Spanish kings, particularly the Philips; 3 excellent portraits of Carews; *Michaelangelo Buonarotti* with his pencil in his hand, remarkably fine, the expression and muscles inimitable; *Theodore Beza*, a good expression, but damaged; the *Regent Earl of Morton*, like that at Dalmahoy; a fine *Cardinal Wolsey* with a collar of SS. The house is old and not worthy notice.

At Dalkeith we saw the Duke of Buccleugh's, a good, habitable house with several portraits, but none remarkably fine. From thence to Yester is 18 miles, the seat of Lord Tweedale. The house, modern and well calculated for a large family, is seated low and surounded with beautyfull and extensive plantations, 6 miles northeast of which lies Haddington, a long, ill-built town, once a place of considerable trade, but much decayed of late years. There are still remaining manufactures of linnen and woolen. There is a bridge of 3 handsome arches over the River Tyne, which is small and not navigable. Here are the remains of an old church <St Mary's>, part of which is converted to the use of divine worship for the inhabitants. The rest is used as a churchyard and enjoys the liberty of being *sub dio*, the roof having long since forsaken the walls. It consists of a nave and 2 narrow isles; in the middle of the cross the buttresses all perpendicular, the arches all plain and pointed; the east window and 2 isles entire. The tower is very handsome and flat at the top; at the top are 3 long, narrow, pointed windows with 2 niches on each side for statues. The church consists of 9 arches on each side, the whole length from south to north (sic) 180 feet, ditto of the cross 90 feet; bredth of the isle 15 feet, ditto of the nave 24 feet.

Close to the town stands an ugly, red, brick house <Amisfield> belonging to Mr Charteris and about 2 miles south a pretty box of Sir J[ohn] Sinclair's <Stevenson>, who has adorned it with large plantations judiciously disposed. 7 miles southeast lies Tyningham, the seat of Lord Haddington, remarkable for the beautyfull and extensive plantations which flourish at the high water mark, notwithstanding they are exposed to sea and the winds on the north and northeast. 3 miles north is Tantallon Castle, held out against James the 5th by the Earl of Angus; it is a heap of ruins.

Here we embarked in a fishing boat to vizit the Bass, a steep rock which stands about 2 miles fom the shore, inaccessible on all sides except one and that narrow and inconvenient, the person ascending being necessitated to climb up by his hands and knees, whilst the sea beats the boat against the rock and if not held tight drives away. Add to this a chance, or rather certainty, of being drowned if by any accident the person should slip. Here was formerly a fortification and 2 or 3 houses, but that is entirely ruined and the only remains are the outwards; the present inhabitants pigeons and solan geese. The latter are nowhere to be found in Britain except this spot, the island of

Ailzye and some of the lesser islands of the Orcades. They come and return in great bodies at a particular season of the year, though many remain there winter and summer, unless driven away by severity of weather. They are said to feed on fish and are reckoned daintyes. At Edinburgh, I was informed, young ones sold for 20 pence sterling per head. They are a large fowl, not quite so big as a goose, web-footed, the bill pointed like a heron. They never disturb them until they have built their nests and then are not easily to be frightened away. They are said to lay but one egg at a time, which they fix by one end to the point of the rock in the middle of the nest and hatch it by holding it fast under one foot. Great profit are made both of the flesh and feathers of the young ones, which are taken out of their nests by one let down the rock by a rope. When young they are ash colored, when old white, except the tip of each wing, which is black. It is remarkable that the old birds always sit on that part of the rock which is white and the pigeons, which are all ash colored or black, on the dark side in order to avoid easy discovery.

Having returned to shore, we returned to Tynningham and thence proceeded by Beel to Yester. In our way thither, being misguided by the stupidity of the country people, my horse fell into a bog, from which he was forced to be drawn by ropes. At Yester land is worth from 20 to 30 years' purchase; arable and pasture lets from 10s to 20s per acre. Manure, dung and lime. Labor from 6d to 8d per day. Thursday 19th < October >. Having travell[ed] 16½ miles over moors and mountains, we came to the miserable town of Lauder, where we saw the antient seat of the Maitlands < Thirlestane Castle >, ruinous and deso-late, and after refreshing our horses proceed[ed] through a country almost as disagreable 9¾ miles to Melrose. Here we crossed the Tweed over a stately bridge of 5 arches. The town is meanly built and has no appearance of trade, though I was told there was a linen manufactory.

Here we saw the remains of the abbey [15] so justly celebrated by all writers. It is said to be one of the first seats of the Culdai, as Fordun says, that is *cultores dei*, but is uncertain when it was founded, probably about the end of the 6th century. The present monastery was founded by King David 1136 and dedicated 1146. It was built in the form of St John's Cross. The roof is very curious, filled with scripture history. Here are buryed the Earl of Douglas and his son James, who were killed at the Battle of Otterburn 1388, in the battle fought with Piercy surnamed Hotspur, afterward Earl of Northumberland. Within, on the north side of the cross, are beautyfull pillars and sculpture as fresh as if lately cut. On the west side of the cross are 2 statues of Peter and Paul. In the middle of it stood the steeple, famous for its architecture, a fourth of it yet standing, the spire entirely destroyed, the roof on the south side still standing and a staircase remarkable for the position of the steps. In the church are many pillars curiously carved, particularly one capital in so masterly and judicious a manner that it [is] called the lace pillar, being supposed to resemble the fineness of the sculpture Flanders lace.

On the outside the east window, where the high altar was, is compleat; it consists of 4 pillars or bars with much curious work between them. On each side are many niches for statues, the pedestals and canopies of which are curiously carved. In one part of the cieling is the creator in miniature. On the southeast are cut out many ludicrous figures, as an angel under the appearance of a highland piper dressed in his plaid; another of a cherub in a flowing bob wig supporting a spout, with many more of the same cast. In the middle of an arch of a window is represented a female head covered with a veil, so admirably executed that it looks like nature. On the south is a window much esteemed for its height and curious workmanship. On the north side of the church was a cloister, of which there is still remaining a close arcade of 7 pointed arches, very curious, over which are carved different flowers, plants, shells, fruit etc, as lillies, grapes, fir cones, scollop shells. The length of the whole is 258 feet, bredth 137½ feet, circumference 943 feet, height of the steeple from the foundation 75 feet. This bulding was defaced by the English under Edward 2, 1322.

The road from Melross is extremely pleasant through a rich well-cultivated country, in many places on the banks of the Tweed, the windings of which afford delightfull prospects, not far distant from which is a handsome house < ?Mertoun > of Mr Scot. The town of Kelso is meanly built; most of the houses are covered with turf or thatch. The inhabitants, by their neighbourhood to England, have so far condescended to imitate them in cleanliness as to cover the inside walls of their rooms with paper, which gives them an air of neatness, and I must do them the justice to add the bedding and linnen is extremely good. But in all other respects they preserve the filthy customs of their countrymen, from which they will not be persuaded to secede. The streets are filled with human excrement from one end to the other, which renders walking unsafe and disagreable.

Friday 20 < th October >. A mile northwest stands Fleurs < Floors >, a large handsome seat belonging to the Duke of Roxburgh, situated on a rising ground at a small distance from the Tweed in a fine sporting country; the plantations are very extensive and ornamental. The family seldom reside there and, the inside of the house not being furnished, no person is permitted to enter to prevent any further reflections being made on the owners for suffering a palace to remain with bare walls. The lands in the neighbourhood are enclosed with mounds of earth planted with quick and a deep ditch towards the road, the enclosures large and trees planted at proper distances. The farmers seem to have adopted enirely the English method of cultivation and thereby improved their lands considerably.

6 miles southeast lyes Coldstream, remarkable for being the place where Charles the 2nd broke his first and oldest regiment of guards for a day and thereby the younger regiment gained the precedence. This was done to comply with the fantastical request of a salacious mistress. Here we forded the Tweed and

on the opposite side entered England again (when my companion in imitation of the eastern people paid homage to his native country by kissing the ground). 16 miles east is Berwick, a large populous town at the mouth of the Tweed, over which is a magnificent bridge of 17 arches. It has a small, bad harbour to which belongs 20 sail of ships from 40 to 150 t[ons] b[urden]. The chief trade is corn and fish, particularly salmon, with which the Tweed abounds. The town hall is a handsome spatious building. The town has once been a place of strength and even now what is styled a fortification, with barracks for troops who garrison it.

In our way to Belford we had a distant view of Holy Island, with the remains of the castle and cathedral. It was once a bishop's see, but was afterwards transferred to Durham; it is called Lindes Farm < Lindisfarne >. The passage to it is over the sands, which are dry at low water, but the tyde unfortunately coming in when we passed it prevented our paying homage to a building of so great antiquity. Belford is a small village 15 [miles] south of Berwick, from which the country is dreary and disagreable. Adjoyning to it Mr Dickson < Dixon > has a handsome new-built house < Belford Hall >.

Our next stage was through a wild, barren moor 14 miles to Alnewick, the county town of Northumberland, tolerably well built. Alnewick Castle, the property of the Earls of Northumberland, remained in ruins untill the present Lord upon coming to it (in right of his wife (daughter to Duke Algernon) begun to repair it in some places and in others to rebuild it in the antient manner. He has already fitted up some rooms with great elegances, one of them 33 feet by 21 feet adorned with coats of arms of the Piercys and other familys with which it is allyed, as the Hastings, Mountagues, Blounts, Godolphins, Nevils and many others. Lord Northumberland at Warkworth has raised his estate in the proportion of from £5 to £10 per annum.

5 miles northwest is Broome Park, a small house belonging to Mr Burrell. It is built on the side of a hill; the lands lye

entirely round it, are all enclosed with quick hedges and planted with trees. The estate is so much improved that it is supposed it will be raised to double the present value when the leases expire. Land in that part [sells at] 30 years' purchase. Arable lets at £0 10s 6d; pasture at £0 15s 0d per acre. Labor from 6d to 8d per day. The antient seat of this family was at Millfield, but the frequent inroads of the Scotch compelled them to remove to a greater distance from the Border. From hence to Morpeth is for the most part through a fine, enclosed and well cultivated country, the enclosures all very extensive, consisting of banks planted with quick and trees defended by a ditch. About 4 miles from Morpeth, in an upland meadow, the first crop of hay remained in the field, October 22nd. Morpeth is a regular town of good extent without trade or manufacture.

From hence I went through a disagreable country 12 miles to Seaton Delaval. The approach is by an avenue a mile in length, scandalously neglected and overgrown in many places with furze. The house was designed by Sir John Vanbrugh, but wears a lighter appearance than any of the aedifices that I ever saw of his building, particularly the wings. The house consists of a square hall, on each [side] of that a good room; in front a handsome saloon filled with family pictures of no great consequence either in point of antiquity or painting. Beyond this, 2 a small skylight passage room, 3 a dineing room adorned with naked figures, 4 a bed chamber through which you are conducted to a drawing room which commands several good views of the sea. The adjacent lands for several miles abound in coal.

5 miles south lyes Tynemouth, remarkable now for its harbor, where the collyers take in their loading at Shields, to which belong 300 sail for the coal trade only, and for the ruins of its castle and little monastry < Tynemouth Priory >. Of the latter the west door remains. At the east end 3 long, narrow, pointed windows in the lower storey; in the second 2 ditto larger and in the uppermost one oval window. At the bottom is a doorway leading to a Lady Chappel, the roof and sides of which is

Tynemouth Priory, Northumberland. Engraved view after painting by L. Clennell, c. 1813. *(Reproduced by permission of the RCAHMS)*

enriched in a curious manner with different figures well preserved.

9 miles up the Tyne stands Newcastle, the great emporium of the north parts of England. I had scarce any opportunity of informing myself of its particular advantages, my stay not exceeding an hour, which was employed in seeing the great church, remarkably large and good. In it are several monuments rather to be admired for their antiquity more than their beauty. The town hall and merchants' [?court] < Guildhall >, both good rooms; in the former the pictures of *Charles* and *James the 2nd*. The town is irregular and resembles other antient towns in bad buildings; the streets extremely narrow, a good key for merchandize, to which the ships lye close, a long bridge over the Tyne, miserably blockaded by bad houses and sheds every 20 yards.

9 miles brought us to Chester le Street, where I saw in the church a series of monuments of the Lumleys [16] from the Conquest to Elizabeth, and with interruptions to George 2nd. It fills up one side of the church and is as follows: 1 Liulphus, the head of the family, descended, as the modern inscription says, from the Anglo-Saxons. This monument is simple; he lyes as with his sword in his hand and not cross legged. 2 Utred, his son, who lived in Henry 1st's time, in the same taste; the heads of both these reclined on cushions. 3 W[illiam] Lumley, his son, lyeing on a cushion with legs crost on a dog, in a coat of armour with helmet, shield and spurs. 4 W[illiam] de Lumley in King John's time, lyeing on his helmet cross legged. 5 W[illiam] Lumley in Henry 3rd's time ditto. 6 Roger, in Edward 1st['s time], lyeing on his helmet. 7 Robert, in Edward ?1[st's time]; legs on a cushion, without a helmet, in his own hair. 8 Sir Marmaduke in ?R[ichar]d 3rd['s time]; legs broken off, in armour and in a praying posture. 9 Ralph, first Lord Lumley, Henry 4th; face covered with his helmet, feet extended on a dog. 10 a mural monument; 2 old men hold a piece of marble with the Lumley arms over it, which mentions it as belonging to his son, Ralph, Lord Lumley. 11 Sir J[ohn] Lumley, ? Henry

3; face and body covered with armour. 12 George Lumley with coronation robes, not well preserved. 13 Sir T[homas] Lumley, Elizabeth; in armor, his legs on a helmet. 14 ?R[ichar]d, Lord Lumley, Henry 8; a more compleat figure than any. 15 John, Lord Lumley, Henry 8, ditto. Besides these 2 or 3 modern monuments not at all remarkable.

From Chester I went to Durham, 6 miles and 10 miles further to Bishop's Aucland, a good market town seated in a pleasant country. Here is a noble palace belonging to the Bishops of Durham. The present bishop has laid out a considerable sum of money in adorning and repairing it. There are some good rooms, particularly a hall 78 feet long, 36 feet broad. In the dineing [room] are the portraits of *Jacob* and the *12 Tribes*, one of them a copy, the original being in the collection of Mr Raymond at Langley in Kent; over the chimney is the *Establishment of the Mass*. There are 2 other pictures well painted in a drawing room and bedchamber adjoyning, viz. *Solomon and the 2 Harlots* and a small *Holy Family*. The chapel was built by Bishop Cozens and is of the following dimensions: length 90 feet, breadth 54 feet, nave 27 feet broad, 2 isles 12 feet broad each; the carving of the skreen is extremely pretty. The isles consist of 7 pointed arches, each 22½ feet wide. The bishop's throne and all other seats within the nave are covered with crimson silk as is the communion table, on which stands an elegant set of plate, silver gilt, the gift of Bishop Cozens.

9 miles off is Stainthrop, near which is Raby Castle, given by King Cnute to the church of Durham, thence came to the Nevils and from them into the Vane family in James the 1st's reign, where it remains. The late Lord Darlington seems to have consumed a very large sum of money in converting this venerable pile of building into a modern house. The grounds on every side are well disposed and kept with the utmost neatness. On one part runs a serpentine canal, which would have a better effect if a considerable formal lake did not render the beautyes of it less strikeing.

Barnard Castle is a good market town standing on the extreme verge of the bishoprick, which is there divided from Yorkshire by the River Tees. Here I saw the ruins of Barnard Castle, built by Bernard Baliol, great grandfather to John Baliol, King of Scots. 3 miles from it lyes Rookby <Rokeby>, the seat of Sir T[homas] Robinson, an extremely pretty house. The rooms in general want height, otherwise good; one indeed is a noble library, length 40 feet 6 inches, height 29, width 27. He has several antique busts and marbles in *alto relievo* of good account. In Rookby plantations the Rivers Tees and Greta join. The gardens appeared to be neglected, for which a ridiculous excuse was made.

From thence I went to Richmond, a pleasant, clean, well-built town. It has the remains of a castle built by Alan, Earl of Bretagne (to whom William the 1st gave the shire of this name), who not dareing to rely on Gilling, his manor, to oppose the ?S[axons] and Danes, fortified it with walls and a castle. In the middle is a high, square building consisting of 5 storeys, the walls almost entire. In the inside is placed a round, Doric pillar about 17 feet high, which could be intended for no other use than that of supporting the floor immediately above it. At one side of the walls are the remains of 2 other square towers. The castle takes up a great space of ground and on one side is almost inaccessible by reason of the River Swale, which flows at the bottom, over which is a stone bridge of 4 arches, and close to it is a good house belonging to Mr Yorke, member for the town. The common people here knit white yarn stockings, which are sent to Holland and sell from 7s to 30s per dozen pair. In Richmond and its libertyes land is [sold for] 30 years' purchase; enclosed pasture near the town [lets] from £2 to £4 per acre, grazeing farms £1 5s 0d, arable £0 12s 0d to £0 15s 0d. Land tax when at 4s they pay 10d; poor rates 12d in the pound; labor 8d winter, 10d summer per day. Manure, lime and dung.

15 miles further lyes Masham, a small market town. About 3 miles from it, at Newton, I was informed the price of land

was 35 years' purchase; arable and pasture let together at £0 10s 0d per acre. Labor 10d per day; land tax £0 1s 6d in the pound. Manure, dung and lime. The country about Masham is remarkably pleasant and commands [a] variety of agreable and extensive prospects. The lands are rich and fertile, but not overburdened wih timber. At Hackfall, an estate of Mr Aislabie's, are the most delightfull amd romantic scenes that are to be met with in these parts; hills covered with timber through which a multitude of small cascades fall murmuring down the rocks into the adjacent vallyes.

At Studley <Royal> are 2 fine pictures, a *Last Supper* by Rubens and a *Circumcision* by Rembrandt, both highly finished. Of the gardens I will not presume to give a description, sensible a task such as that would be too difficult an undertaking for so weak a pen as mine. Rippon is a neat, well-built town; wool is the chief trade. The cathedral is a handsome building consisting of 2 towers at the west end, 2 isles, a cross with a tower in the middle. The arches of the windows in the choir differ from each [other], some being round, others pointed, others trefoiled. The chapter house hath 2 pillars in the middle. This whole aedifice is kept in good repair. In a vault in the nave close to the cross is the famous needle of St Wilfred, remarkable for proving the chastity of such females who ventured to undergo the tryal, through which if they had transgressed they were supposed to be unable to pass, but if innocent with great ease, a trick of those religious juglers, the monks, who by this contrivance had frequent opportunities of indulging their lascivious eyes; at least, in the view of such things as by their vows they ought to abstain from, though their age might give them an appetite.

Boroughbridge is a poor, mean town without trade or manufacture, except the accidental branch of electioneering. 12 miles south is Wetherby, another place of small importance. Here are mills for grinding rape seed and others for all sorts of dyeing woods. The process of the first is to bruise the seed sufficiently, then put a proper quantity into a pan to be warmed over the fire, which when heated to a certain degree is placed in small bags, pressed close and filled as tight as possible, when they are fixed in a sort of frame and wedges being drove in on one side of the bag compresses it violently and by that means extracts the oyl. The rape dust is sold to the farmer at 10s per quarter and is by them esteemed highly serviceable to land sowed with barley and wheat; on the former to be laid in the spring, the latter in autumn. But as it is of a hot nature it will not be effectual unless rain falls after it is thrown on the fields; I own I am a a loss to conceive how the expence can be answered. The dyeing wood is cut and pounded at once by the same engine which makes it ready for the use of the dyers. Arable land about the town [lets] from 6s to 16s, pasture from 2s 6d to £3 per acre.

Ferrybridge lyes 16 miles south. In my way thither I went a mile out of the road to see Bramham Hall, Mr Lane's. The outside appearance is grand, to which the inside is in no wise answerable. The plantations are extensive, the gardens, in the old taste, too formal to be agreable. The vale through which I passed at the entrance to Ferrybridge is extremely beautyfull; it extends several miles. Through it runs the River Are < Aire >, navigable above the town, and the neighbouring hills are lined with towns and villages. Land [sells at] 30 years' purchase. Meadow lets at 20s, arable at 10s per acre. Labor 12d winter, 1s 6d summer per day.

Doncaster is seated in a fine, sporting country, but rather too flat. The town is well built, the streats spatious and beautyfull. It is very populous and carryes on a considerable inland trade in corn and other articles of less importance. The river flows close to the north side and is navigable for small vessels. The market place, or rather shambles, for butchers' meat etc is built of freestone remarkably neat. The corporation have expended upwards of £8000 in erecting a mansion house and fitted it up in the most elegant manner, particularly the 2 chimneypieces in the great room, which consist of black and white marble. This room is 60 feet long, 30 wide and 30 high. The church is a handsome, Gothic aedifice [and] consists of a nave, 2 isles and a cross. In it are some antient monumental gravestones adorned with coats of arms on the sides and ends, but no inscription. The soil near the town and many miles south of it is sand, which is sowed with turnips to improve it.

Bautry is of no great importance either for trade or manufacture and only known by being the next stage from Doncaster. At Barnby on the moor the enclosures are remarkably large and the sandy soil considerably improved by turnips. By the want of timber in the hedgerows or even trees of any sort, I should imagine the enclosures of a late date. Tuxford is the next stage, a small village of no note. Newark is filled with houses of the better class, is well stored wih good inns; on the north are considerable ruins of an old castle. The church is a venerable building [and] consists of a nave and 2 isles. On the north side of the town flows the Trent, over which is erected a high bridge.

Grantham I have mentioned in the former part of the book, to which I have only to add its church, which consists of a nave and 2 isles, the inside well fitted up, but like the kirks in Scotland too much crouded with gallerys, which spoyl the view of the isles; the spire is extremely handsome. Stamford and the other towns to Ware I have already noted (making 63 miles), except Puckeridge, where I received the following information. Land in the neighbourhood sells from 20 to 25 years' purchase. Arable and meadow let together at 6s to 14s per acre. Manure, dung, mould and chalk. Labor the whole year 1s and beer, in harvest more. The farms run from £20 to £200 per annum. Land tax 3s 6d in the pound; now it is by Act of Parliament at 4s poor rates 3s in the pound.

NOTES

1. The Cave at Royston.

   In 1742 a mysterious cave decorated with sculptured figures was discovered beneath the old butter-market at Royston. The following year William Stukeley, the antiquary, published an account of the discovery in a pamphlet entitled *Palaeographia Britannica No. 1*. Stukeley argued that the carvings were allegorical representations of historical events of the twelfth and thirteenth centuries and that the cave was the hermitage of Lady Roisia de Vere, the supposed foundress of Royston. The cave is still there, but current opinion associates it with the Knights Templar of Baldock and ascribes the carvings to the 13th century.

   Piggott, Stuart, *William Stukeley* (2nd ed. 1985), 120–1.

2. Mr Cooper Thornhill.

   Cooper Thornhill, landlord of the Bell Inn at Stilton, was responsible for popularising Stilton cheese, although much of the cheese that he sold under that name seems, in fact, to have been made for him by relatives in Leicestershire.

   Hartley, Dorothy, *Food in England* (1954), 487; Victoria County History of England, *Huntingdonshire* iii (1936), 222.

3. The cupola at Beverley Minster.

   Early eighteenth-century repairs to the minster included the replacement of the lantern over the central tower by an ogival cupola in 1721–3. Burrell was not the only critic of the design (probably by Hawksmoor), and the cupola was removed in 1824.

   Victoria County History, *Yorkshire, East Riding*, vi (1989), 234; Poulson, George, *Beverlac, or the Antiquities of the Town of Beverley* (1829), 679.

4. Inscriptions at Castle Howard.

   Eight Latin inscriptions copied by Burrell at Castle Howard are noted separately on folio 45 of the manuscript. They form part of a collection of classical antiquities, many of which were acquired by the 4th Earl of Carlisle, who died a few weeks after Burrell's visit. All but one of the inscriptions are still preserved at Castle Howard.

   Information from the Hon. Simon Howard, Castle Howard.

5. Carved Stone, Annan.

Burrell seems to be the earliest traveller to furnish a description of this stone, which was subsequently recorded by Pococke, Pennant and others. The Royal Commission on the Ancient and Historical Monuments of Scotland (RCAHMS) gives the following reading: ROBERT DE BRVS/ COUNTE DE CA/[RRIK] ET SENZ[N]U/[R] <i.e. seigneur> DU VAL D[E AN]N/ AND 1300/ and suggests that the date had been added to the original inscription. The stone is now preserved within the Council Chamber of Annan Town Hall.

[Kemp, D. W., ed.], *Tours in Scotland, 1747, 1750, 1760 by Richard Pococke* – (Scottish History Society, 1887), 35; [Pennant, Thomas], *A Tour in Scotland* (5th ed. 1790), ii, 96; RCAHMS, *Inventory of Dumfriesshire* (1920), 3; *Transactions of the Dumfries and Galloway Natural History and Antiquarian Society*, 3rd series, iv (1915–6), 69–84.

6. "those 2nd race of the Stephens's, Messrs Robert and Andrew Foulis".

   In comparing the Foulis brothers to the well-known Parisian family of sixteenth-century scholar printers of the name of Estienne, or Stephens, Burrell could hardly have paid them a higher compliment.

   Glaister, G. A., *Glossary of the Book*, 2nd. ed. (1979), 163.

7. Professors Moor and Smyth.

   James Moor, a distinguished classical scholar, held the chair of Greek at Glasgow University from 1747 to 1774. The chair of Humanity was occupied from 1754 to 1773 by George Muirhead and it is likely that Burrell's second befriender was, in fact, the celebrated Adam Smith, who was at that time professor of Moral Philosophy.

   Coutts, James, *A History of the University of Glasgow* (1909), 215–224.

8. Glen Almond.

   Andrew Rutherford's *An Exact Plan of His Majesty's Great Roads through the Highlands of Scotland* was published in 1745. Burrell may have carried a copy with him.

9. The Monastery of Kinnegary.

   This establishment, usually referred to as the monastery of Loch Tay, was an uncertain foundation of the Augustinian order.

   Cowan, Ian B. and Easson, David E., *Medieval Religious Houses of Scotland* (1976), 98–9.

10. John Campbell, schoolmaster at Airds.

John Campbell's description of Iona was also used by a number of later writers, including Pococke, Forbes and Buchan, all of whom give slightly differing versions of it. The original manuscript was in the possession of Sir Arthur Mitchell in 1901, but its present whereabouts are unknown.

Royal Commission on the Ancient and Historical Monuments of Scotland, *Inventory of Argyll*, iv Iona (1982), 150, 275, 279, giving references to other users; Mitchell, Sir Arthur, "A List of Travels, Tours – etc. relating to Scotland", in *Proceedings of the Society of Antiquaries of Scotland*, xxxv (1900–1), 504.

11. Cormac Macart.

In fact, Keating relates that Cormac MacAirt was buried at Ros na Riogh, in the Boyne Valley (County Meath). The site was subsequently visited by St Columba.

Keating, Geoffrey, *History of Ireland* (Irish Texts Society, 1902–14), ii, 347–9, iv, 132.

12. Cairnbane.

This structure, situated at Portnacroish on the north side of Loch Laich, was probably a chambered cairn of the neolithic period. Two years after Burrell's visit Bishop Pococke managed to enter the cairn and explore what seem to have been two roofed cells. No traces of the cairn are now visible.

[Kemp, D. W. ed.], *Tours in Scotland 1747, 1750, 1760 by Richard Pococke* – (Scottish History Society, 1887), 95; Royal Commission on the Ancient and Historical Monuments of Scotland, *Inventory of Argyll*, ii Lorn (1975), 6, 43.

13. Macbeth's Castle, Forres.

The text is corrupt at this point, but the reference is probably to the royal castle of Forres, which Shakespeare associates with Macbeth. The castle stood on the west side of the town, not the north, but Burrell's sense of direction is weak in this section of the tour and he makes a similar mistake at Elgin. Sir William Dunbar, 2nd Bt. of Hempriggs (d. 1793), married Elizabeth, heiress of the Dunbars of Westfield, who had a long association with the castle. The building on the castle hill seems, in fact, to have been commenced by William Dawson, provost of Forres, in the early years of the eighteenth century, but left unfinished.

Douglas, Sir Robert, *The Baronage of Scotland* (1798), 122; Shaw, Lachlan, *The History of the Province of Moray* (new edition by Gordon, J. F. S., 1882), ii, 171; Douglas, Robert, *Annals of the Royal Burgh of Forres* (1934), 523–5.

14. John Roy Stuart.
Colonel John Roy Stewart served as one of the Jacobite commanders during the Young Pretender's campaign.
Duke, W., *Prince Charles Edward and the Forty-five* (1938), 91.
15. Melrose Abbey.
Burrell probably gained his information about Melrose from the Rev. A. Milne's *A description of the parish of Melrose* – first published in 1748. He seems to have been unaware that the early monastery was situated at Old Melrose, some 4km east of the medieval abbey.
16. Lumley Monument, Chester-le-Street
This remarkable collection of effigies was assembled by John, Lord Lumley, as an act of family piety during the 1590s. The majority of the effigies are Elizabethan imitations, but five are genuine, although in some cases wrongly attributed.
Fordyce, William, *The History and Antiquities of the County Palatine of Durham* (1855–7), ii, 602–3; Milner, Edith, *Records of the Lumleys of Lumley Castle* (1904), 75; Pevsner, Nikolaus and Williamson, Elizabeth, *County Durham* (2nd edition 1983), 127.

Index

Abercorn Castle (West Lothian), 74
Aberdeen (Aberdeenshire), 105–6;
  Marischal College, 105; Seaton
  House, 105; University, 105
Aberdour, Sholto Charles Douglas,
  Lord (aft. 14th Earl of Morton),
  79
Aberfeldy (Perthshire), 67
Aberlemno (Angus), 108
Abernethy (Morayshire), 99
Achnacarry (Inverness-shire), 94
Adam, William, architect, 73, 105
Ailsa Craig (Ayrshire), 55, 120
Airds (Argyll), 88–90; House, 89
Aislabie, William, 129
Alnwick (Northumberland), 123;
  Castle, 123
Amisfield House (East Lothian), 119
Ancaster (Lincolnshire), 29
Ancaster & Kesteven, Peregrine
  Bertie, 3rd Duke of, 27
Annan (Dumfriesshire), 48
Annandale, George Johnstone, 3rd
  Marquess of, 40
Anstruther, Sir John, 2nd Bt. of
  Anstruther, 116
Antrim (Co. Antrim), 52–3
Arbroath (Angus), 111; abbey,
  111–12
Argyll, Archibald Campbell, 3rd
  Duke of, 84
Atholl, James Murray, 2nd Duke
  of, 69
Ayr (Ayrshire), 55–7

Baldock (Hertfordshire), 25

Ballantrae (Ayrshire), 54
Ballinbreich Castle (Fife), 111
Ballymoney (Co. Antrim), 53–4
Banff (Banffshire), 104–5; Castle,
  104
Bargany, (Ayrshire), 55
Barker, Captain, 95
Barnard Castle (Co. Durham), 128
Barnby Moor (Nottinghamshire), 131
Barton-upon-Humber
  (Lincolnshire), 31
Bass Rock (East Lothian), 119–20
Bawtry (Yorkshire), 131
Belfast (Co. Antrim), 50–2
Belford (Northumberland), 123;
  Hall, 123
Belton House (Lincolnshire), 28
Belvoir Castle (Leicestershire), 28
Berwick-upon-Tweed
  (Northumberland), 123
Beverley (Yorkshire), 33–4; minster,
  33
Biel (East Lothian), 120
Bishop Auckland (Co. Durham),
  127
Black Hambleton (Yorkshire), 37
Blackness Castle (West Lothian), 74
Blair, Mr., 48
Blair Atholl (Perthshire), 69–70,
  Castle, 69–70
Blairvochy (Stirlingshire), 82
Bonhill (Dunbartonshire), 80
Boroughbridge (Yorkshire), 129
Bowes, George, 44
Braco, William Duff, 1st Baron (aft.
  1st Earl Fife), 104

Braemar (Aberdeenshire), 97
Bramham Hall (Yorkshire), 130
Brampton (Cumberland), 45
Breadalbane, John Campbell, 3rd
Earl of, 67, 76, 84
Brechin (Angus), 107-8
Brocklesby (Lincolnshire), 30
Brodie, Alexander, of Brodie, 101
Brodie Castle (Morayshire), 101
Broome Park (Northumberland),
123
Bruce, Sir John see Hope
Buccleuch, Henry Scott, 3rd Duke
of, 74, 118
Buchanan House (Stirlingshire), 80
Buckingham, George Villiers, 5th
Duke of, 36
Buckingham, John Sheffield, 6th
Duke of, 42
Burdon, John, 43
Burghley House
(Northamptonshire), 27
Burntisland (Fife), 116
Burrell, Mr., of Ryhall, 27
Burrell, Bryan, 123
Burrell, Sir William, 2nd Bt.;
passim; life, 5-6; northern tour,
8-18
Burrell family, 5-6

Cairnbane (Argyll), 93
Cairndow (Argyll), 83
Camden, William, antiquary, 8, 14,
92, 100
Campbell, Mr., 59
Campbell, Donald, of Airds, 89
Campbell, Dugald, 88
Campbell, Sir Duncan, of Lochnell,
86, 88
Campbell, John, schoolmaster at
Airds, 10, 90
Campbell, Mungo, 94-5
Campbell, Niall, of Dunstaffnage,
86
Campbell, Robert, of Asknish, 83

Carlisle, Henry Howard, 4th Earl
of, 45
Carlisle family, 38
Carlisle (Cumberland), 45-6, 48
Carr, Ralph, 44
Castle Gordon (Morayshire), 102
Castle Grant (Morayshire), 99-100
Castle Howard (Yorkshire), 38
Castle Huntly (Perthshire), 109, 111
Castle Kennedy (Wigtownshire), 50
Castle Lyon see Castle Huntly
Castle Stewart (Inverness-shire), 97
Caxton (Cambridgeshire), 26
Charteris, Francis, of Amisfield, 119
Chatelherault (Lanarkshire), 65
Chester-le-Street (Co. Durham), 44,
126-7
Chesterton (Huntingdonshire), 27
Cholmley, Mr., 41
Cochran, Major, 62
Cocken (Co. Durham), 44
Coldstream (Berwickshire), 122
Colquhoun, Sir James, 1st Bt. of
Luss, 80
Colsterworth (Lincolnshire), 28
Connel (Argyll), 86
Corby (Cumberland), 46
Corby Common (Lincolnshire), 28
Cosin, John, Bp. of Durham, 127
Crawford, Mr., of Errol, 111
Crieff (Perthshire), 66-7
Cundum, Colonel, 34
Cullen (Banffshire), 102, 104;
House, 102, 104
Culloden House (Inverness-shire), 97
Cust, Lady (?widow of Sir Richard
Cust, 2nd Bt.), 28

Dailly (Ayrshire), 55
Dalkeith (Midlothian), 74-5;
House, 74-5, 118
Dalmahoy House (Midlothian), 79
Dalnacardoch (Perthshire), 68
Dalrymple, Sir David, 3rd Bt. of
Hailes, 75

138

Dalrymple, John (aft. 5th Earl of Stair), 50
Darlington, Henry Vane, 2nd Earl of, 127
Darnaway Castle (Morayshire), 98
Defoe, Daniel, 14
Denoon Castle (Angus), 113
Deskford, James Ogilvie, Lord (aft. 6th Earl of Findlater), 104
Dixon, Abraham, 123
Donaghadee (Co. Down), 50, 54
Doncaster (Yorkshire), 130-1
Drum, The (Midlothian), 75
Drumlanrig Castle (Dumfriesshire), 48-9
Drummond Castle (Perthshire), 66
Ducarel, Andrew Coltee, antiquary, 7-8
Duff, The Hon. James, 104
Duff House (Banffshire), 104-5
Dumbarton Castle,(Dunbartonshire), 79, 82
Dumfries (Dumfriesshire), 48-9
Dunbar, Sir William, 2nd Bt. of Hempriggs, 101
Duncombe, Sir Charles, 36
Duncombe, Thomas, 36
Duncombe Park (Yorkshire), 36
Dundee, (Angus), 108, 113
Dundonald, Thomas Cochrane, 8th Earl of, 59
Dunkeld (Perthshire), 68, 70; House, 70
Dunnottar Castle (Kincardineshire), 106
Duniphail Castle (Morayshire), 99
Dunstaffnage Castle (Argyll), 86, 88, 94
Durham (Co. Durham), 43-4, 127
Dysart (Fife), 116

Easdale (Argyll), 83
East, Mr., 56
East Park (Midlothian), 75
Edinburgh (Midlothian), 74-9;
Castle, 66, 75, 79; Cross, 75;
Exchange, 76; Heriot's Hospital, 77; Holyroodhouse, 76-7; Royal Infirmary, 77; St Giles Church, 78; University, 78
Eglinton Castle (Ayrshire), 57
Elgin (Morayshire), 101-2
Elie (Fife), 116
Elphinstone (East Lothian), 75
Errol (Perthshire), 111
Erskine, Thomas, 65
Exeter, Brownlow Cecil, 9th Earl of, 27

Fairfax of Emley, Charles Fairfax, 9th Viscount, 36
Ferrybridge (Yorkshire), 130
Fieres see Foyers
Finchale Abbey (Co. Durham), 44
Findlater, James Ogilvie, 5th Earl of, 102
Finlarig Castle (Perthshire), 68
Floors Castle (Roxburghshire), 122
Fochabers (Morayshire), 102
Forbes, Duncan, of Culloden, 97
Forbes, John, of Culloden, 97
Forbes, Robert, Bp. of Caithness & Ross, 10, 17
Forfar (Angus), 108
Forres (Morayshire), 100-1
Fort Augustus (Inverness-shire), 95
Fort George (Inverness-shire), 97-8
see also Inverness
Fort William (Inverness-shire), 82, 85, 94
Foulis, Andrew, 63
Foulis, Robert, 63
Foyers (Inverness-shire), 95-6
Frazer, Mr., of Foyers, 96

Gale, Samuel, antiquary, 7
Giant's Causeway (Co. Antrim), 53-4
Gibbs, James, architect, 105
Gibside (Co. Durham), 44

Gilling (Yorkshire), 128; Castle, 36
Girvan (Ayrshire), 55
Glamis (Angus), 108–9, 111, 113;
    Castle, 109
Glanford Brigg (Lincolnshire), 30
Glasgow (Lanarkshire), 59–66;
    Castle, 62; Cathedral, 61; Foulis
    Academy, 63; St Andrews
    Church, 60–1; University, 62–3
Glasgow, John Boyle, 3rd Earl of, 57
Glenluce (Wigtownshire), 49
Glentworth Hall (Lincolnshire), 30
Gordon, Alexander, antiquary, 14,
    16, 108
Gordon, Alexander Gordon, 4th
    Duke of, 102
Gordon Castle (Morayshire), 102
Granby, John Manners, Marquess
    of, 28
Grant, Sir Ludovick, 7th Bt. of
    Grant, 99–100
Grantham (Lincolnshire), 28–9
Greenock (Renfrewshire), 57–8
Grimsthorpe (Lincolnshire), 28
Guisborough (Yorkshire), 42

Hackfall (Yorkshire), 129
Hackness (Yorkshire), 40
Haddington, Thomas Hamilton, 7th
    Earl of, 78, 119
Haddington (East Lothian), 118–19
Hamilton, James Hamilton, 6th
    Duke of, 65
Hamilton, James Hamilton, 7th
    Duke of, 76
Hamilton, John, of Bargany, 55
Hamilton (Lanarkshire), 65; House,
    64–5
Hardwick Hall (Co. Durham), 43
Hardwicke, Philip Yorke, 1st Earl
    of, 25
Harlow Hill (Northumberland), 45
Heathcote, Sir John, 2nd Bt. of
    Normanton, 26
Helmsley (Yorkshire), 36–7

Hetton (Co. Durham), 44
Hoby, Sir Thomas, 4th Bt., 40
Honington (Lincolnshire), 29
Hope, Sir John Bruce, 7th Bt. of
    Craighall, 72
Hopetoun, John Hope, 2nd Earl of,
    74
Hopetoun House (West Lothian),
    72–4
Horsley, John, antiquary, 14
Hotham, Sir Charles, 6th Bt., 8, 33
Hotham, Sir John, 1st Bt., 32
Houghton-le-Spring (Co. Durham),
    44
House of Nairne (Perthshire), 71
Howard, Philip, 46
Hull (Yorkshire), 31–3
Huntingdon (Huntingdonshire), 26

Icolmkill see Iona
Inchconnachan, Loch Lomond, 80
Inchgalbraith, Loch Lomond, 80
Inchlonaig, Loch Lomond, 80
Inchmurrin, Loch Lomond, 80
Inchtavannach, Loch Lomond, 80
Innes, George, 78
Inveraray (Argyll), 83–5; Castle,
    83–4
Inverbervie (Kincardineshire), 106
Invergarry Castle (Inverness-shire),
    95
Inverkeithing (Fife), 72
Inverlochy Castle (Inverness-shire),
    94
Inverness (Inverness-shire), 96; Fort
    George, 96
Iona (Argyll), 89–93; abbey, 90–2;
    nunnery, 93; Reilig Odhrain, 92
Irvine (Ayrshire), 57

Jones, Inigo, architect, 109

Keating, Dr. Geoffrey, 92
Keith family, Earls Marischal, 105–6
Kelburn Castle (Ayrshire), 57

Kelso (Roxburghshire), 122
Kenmore (Perthshire), 67–8
Kidd, Captain, 116
Kiliwhimen (Inverness-shire), 95
Killiecrankie (Perthshire), 70
Kilsyth (Stirlingshire), 65
Kilwinning (Ayrshire), 57
Kinghorn (Fife), 117
Kinloss Abbey (Morayshire), 100
Kinnegary *see* Loch Tay Monastery
Kinross (Kinross-shire), 71–2;
   House, 72

Laggan (Inverness-shire), 95
Lane, George Fox, 130
Langley Park (Kent), 127
Largs (Ayrshire), 57
Leith (Midlothian), 117
Leuchars (Fife), 113–14
Lincoln (Lincolnshire), 29, 31, 35
Lindisfarne (Northumberland), 123
Lochaber (Inverness-shire), 94
Loch Lomond, 80
Lochnell House (Argyll), 88
Loch Tay Monastery, (Perthshire), 68
Logie House (Morayshire), 98–9
Lorn Furnace (Argyll), 86
Lough Neagh, 53
Lumley Castle (Co. Durham), 44
Lumley family, 126–7
Luss (Dunbartonshire), 80, 82

Macbeth's Castle, Forres (Moray-
   shire), 101
Macdonnell, Alexander, of
   Glengarry, 95
McKune, Mr., 48
Malton (Yorkshire), 37–8
Marnham (Nottinghamshire), 29
Masham (Yorkshire), 128–9
Massereene, Clotworthy
   Skeffington, 2nd Earl of, 52–3
Meigle (Perthshire), 108–9
Melrose (Roxburghshire); 120–2;
   Abbey, 120–2

Menzies, Sir Robert, 3rd Bt. of
   Castle Menzies, 67
Mertoun House (Berwickshire), 122
Middleton, Mr., of Seaton, 105
Millfield (Northumberland), 124
Montagu, John Montagu, 2nd Duke
   of, 39
Montrose, William Graham, 2nd
   Duke of, 80
Montrose (Angus), 106–7
Moor, Professor James, 63
Moray, James Stewart, 8th Earl of,
   97–8
Moray, Margaret Wemyss,
   Countess of, 100
Morpeth (Northumberland), 124
Morton, James Douglas, 13th Earl
   of, 79
Moy House (Morayshire), 98–100
Muckairn (Argyll), 86
Mulgrave Castle (Yorkshire), 42

Nairn, John Nairn, 3rd Lord, 71
Nairn (Nairnshire), 98
Nairne House *see* House of Nairne
Naworth Castle (Cumberland), 45
Neville family, 127
Newark (Nottinghamshire), 131
Newbattle (Midlothian), 118
Newburn (Northumberland), 45
Newcastle upon Tyne
   (Northumberland), 45, 126
New Hailes (Midlothian), 75
Newton (Yorkshire), 128–9
Newton Stewart (Wigtownshire),
   49
Northumberland, Hugh Percy
   (form. Smithson), 2nd Earl of, 123

Old Aberdeen *see* Aberdeen
Old Meldrum (Aberdeenshire), 105
O'Neill, Charles, of Shane's Castle,
   53

Paisley (Renfrewshire), 58–9

Panmure, James Maule, 4th Earl of, 107
Panmure House (Angus), 112–13
Panmure of Forth, William Maule, Earl of, 107,112
Pelham, Charles, 30–1
Pennant, Thomas, antiquary, 17
Perth, Edward Drummond, 6th (titular) Duke of, 66
Perth (Perthshire), 71
Phipps, Constantine (aft. Baron Mulgrave), 42
Phipps, Lady Lepell (aft. Baroness Mulgrave), 42
Pigott, Robert, 27
Pococke, Richard, Bp. of Ossory, 8, 10, 16
Port Glasgow (Renfrewshire), 58–9, 82
Port Patrick (Wigtownshire), 50, 54
Port Sonachan (Argyll), 86
Portsoy (Banffshire), 104
Puckridge (Hertfordshire), 131

Queensberry, Charles Douglas, 3rd Duke of, 48
Queensferry, North (Fife), 72
Queensferry, South (West Lothian), 72

Raby Castle (Co. Durham), 127
Rainton (Co. Durham), 44
Raymond, Jones, 127
Richardson, John, provost of Inveraray, 83
Richmond (Yorkshire), 128
Rievaulx Abbey (Yorkshire), 37
Ripon (Yorkshire), 129
Robinson, Sir Thomas, 1st Bt., 128
Rokeby Hall (Yorkshire), 128
Roslin (Midlothian), 117–18
Rosyth Castle (Fife), 72
Rothes, John Leslie, 9th Earl of, 111
Roxburghe, John Ker, 3rd Duke of, 122

Royston (Hertfordshire), 25
Rudha Garbh (Argyll), 88
Rutherford, Andrew, 12, 66
Rutland, John Manners, 3rd Duke of, 28
Ryhall (Rutland), 27

St. Andrews (Fife), 114–16; cathedral, 115; Holy Trinity Church 115–16; St. Salvator's College, 114
St. Clair, General James, 117
St. Quinton, Sir William, 4th Bt., 38
Scampston (Yorkshire), 38–9
Scarborough, Richard Lumley-Saunderson, 4th Earl of, 30
Scarborough (Yorkshire), 38–40
Scone Palace (Perthshire), 71
Scott, Walter, of Harden, 122
Seaton Delaval (Northumberland), 124
Sedgefield (Co. Durham), 43
Settrington (Yorkshire), 39
Shane's Castle (Co. Antrim), 53
Shields, North (Northumberland), 124
Sinclair, Sir John, 6th Bt. of Stevenson, 119
Skinner, Colonel William, 97
Smith, Professor Adam, 63
Somerset, Algernon Seymour, 7th Duke of, 123
Somerville, James Somerville, 12th Lord, 75
Spital-in-the-Street (Lincolnshire), 30
Staindrop (Co. Durham), 127
Stair, John Dalrymple, 2nd Earl of, 50
Staithes (Yorkshire), 42
Stamford (Lincolnshire), 27, 131
Stanwix Bank (Cumberland), 46
Stevenson, Major, 78
Stevenson (East Lothian), 119
Stewart, Mr., 78
Stewart, Mr. (aft. Sir John

Shaw-Stewart, 4th Bt. of
  Blackhall and Greenock), 58
Stewart, Colonel John Roy, 102
Stewart, Sir Michael, 3rd Bt. of
  Blackhall, 58
Stilton (Huntingdonshire), 26
Stirling (Stirlingshire), 65–6, 68–9;
  Castle, 65–6, 82; Mar's Lodging, 65
Stockton (Co. Durham), 42–3
Stonehaven (Kincardineshire), 106
Stormont, David Murray, 7th
  Viscount, 71
Stranraer (Wigtownshire), 49, 54
Strathmore & Kinghorne, John
  Lyon, 9th Earl of, 44, 108
Strathmore & Kinghorne, Patrick
  Lyon, 3rd Earl of, 109
Studley Royal (Yorkshire), 129
Stukeley, William, antiquary, 14,
  16, 25
Sueno's Stone, Forres, 100
Sutton (Yorkshire), 32
Swalwell (Co. Durham), 45
Sydenham, Sir Philip, 3rd Bt., 40
Symonds, John, 6–7, 9–10, 12, 26

Tantallon Castle (East Lothian), 119
Tarbet (Dunbartonshire), 82
Taylor, Dr., John, 7
Taymouth Castle (Perthshire), 67–8
Thirlestane Castle (Berwickshire),
  120
Thompson, Mr., 31

Thompson, Tindall, 39
Thornhill, Cooper, 26
Tirefour Broch (Argyll), 89
Trapaud, Alexander,
  deputy-governor of Fort
  Augustus, 95
Tulloch, Mr., of Logie, 98
Turriff (Aberdeenshire), 105
Tuxford (Nottinghamshire), 131
Tweeddale, John Hay, 4th Marquess
  of, 118
Tyndrum (Argyll), 85
Tynemouth Priory
  (Northumberland), 124, 126
Tyninghame (East Lothian), 119

Vanbrugh, Sir John, architect, 38,
  124

Wade's Hut (Inverness-shire), 96
Wansford (Northamptonshire), 27
Ware (Hertfordshire), 131
Warkworth (Northumberland), 123
Weem (Perthshire), 67
Wetherby (Yorkshire), 129
Whitby (Yorkshire), 40–2 ; Abbey
  House, 41
Wimpole (Cambridgeshire), 25

Yester (East Lothian), 118, 120
York (Yorkshire), 34–6; Castle, 35;
  minster, 34–5
Yorke, Thomas, 128